Anonymous

Report of the Dutchess County and Poughkeepsie Sanitary Fair, Held at Sanitary Hall,

in the city of Poughkeepsie, from March 15 to March 19, 1864

Anonymous

Report of the Dutchess County and Poughkeepsie Sanitary Fair, Held at Sanitary Hall,
in the city of Poughkeepsie, from March 15 to March 19, 1864

ISBN/EAN: 9783337308056

Printed in Europe, USA, Canada, Australia, Japan

Cover: Foto ©ninafisch / pixelio.de

More available books at **www.hansebooks.com**

REPORT

OF THE

DUTCHESS COUNTY & POUGHKEEPSIE

SANITARY FAIR,

HELD AT

SANITARY HALL,

IN THE

CITY OF POUGHKEEPSIE,

From March 15 to March 19, 1864.

POUGHKEEPSIE:

PRINTED BY PLATT & SCHRAM, DAILY EAGLE OFFICE.

1864.

Officers.

—o—

PRESIDENT:
MRS. JAMES WINSLOW.

VICE PRESIDENTS:

MRS. THOS. L. DAVIES,   MRS. B. J. LOSSING,
" G. C. BURNAP,   " WM. S. MORGAN,
" GEORGE INNIS,   " JOHN THOMPSON,
MRS. DR. BEADLE.

SECRETARY:
Mrs. CHARLES H. RUGGLES.

TREASURER:
Miss SARAH M. CARPENTER.

The President, Vice Presidents, Secretary and Treasurer, with the
following Ladies, form the EXECUTIVE COMMITTEE:

MRS. CHARLES H. SWIFT,   MRS. LEGRAND DODGE,
" VAN VALKENBURGH,   " C. W. TOOKER,
MRS. HAYDOCK.

MANAGERS:

Mrs. David L. Jones,	Mrs. D. H. Wright,	Mrs. Dr. Dubois,
" Wm. A. Davies,	Miss Merritt,	" Dr. Fowler,
" W. H. Crosby,	Mrs. Dr. Robertson,	Miss Julia Crosby,
" Tho. Wickes,	Miss Julia Dibble,	" E. Thomas,
" Dr. Hoffman,	Mrs. G. I. Vincent,	Mrs. Geo. W. Sterling,
" F. Davis,	" Van Aulen,	" I. Platt,
" Oscar Fowler,	" Jas. Reynolds,	" Weddle,
" Henry Stevens,	" Henry D. Varick,	" Van Cleef,
" Theo. Trivett,	" Wm. Schram,	" North,
" John Sherman,	" A. Bourman,	" G. T. Brown,
" Ryder,	" Geo. Wilkinson,	" Dr. Hasbrouck,
" Parish,	Miss Babcock,	Miss Jane Varick,
" J. F. Hull,	Mrs. Nathan Sandford,	Mrs Henry Swift,
" T. Gregory,	" Robert R. Taylor,	" J. P. Adriance,
" L. Leggett,	" Major Patton,	" John Robinson,
" L. M. Ferris,	" J. B. Jewett,	" Geo. Cornwell,
" E. Beach,	" Joseph Wright,	" Geo. B. Lent,
" Prof. Eastman,	" G. Van Kleeck,	" R. W. James
" E. Marshall,	" Jas. Wilkinson,	Miss Phinney,
" A. Wright,	" Henry W. Shaw,	Mrs. Cogswell,
" Ellsworth,	" C. Van Wyck,	" J. G. Wood,
" J. D. Hegar,	" F. Elting,	" Fredricks.

NAMES OF MANAGERS FROM THE COUNTY.

appointed by the Secretary, and who accepted their appointments:

Red Hook—Mrs. John Aspinwall, Mrs. Amenia—Miss Kate Powers.
John M. Lewis, Mrs. John Burd. Washington—Miss Hattie Coffin, Mrs.
Fishkill Landing—Mrs Wm Verplanck, Milton Hull.
Mrs. R. P. Hart, Mrs. E. P. Deckie. Dover—Mrs. Asa Wright, Mrs. Z. Radd.
East Fishkill—Miss D. Horton. Mrs. Belden.
Wappinger's Falls—Miss Jos. Fraulker, Pleasant Valley—Mrs. Geo. Jones.
Pine Plains—Mrs. Elliott Woodin Beekman—Miss Alma Sterling, Miss
New Hackensack—Miss Knapp. Mary Noxon.
Marbletsville—Miss Lucy B. Coffin. Pawling—Mrs. Helen M. Tabor.
LaGrange—Mrs. Peter I. Sleight, Mrs. Clinton—Mrs. Wesley Butts.
Van Benschoten. Stanford—Mrs. Issue G. Sands.

From the Board of Managers the Cashiers and Committees were chosen.

List of Committees.

— o —

ADVISORY COMMITTEE:

William Thompson,   C. J. Buckingham,
T. B. Costar,   Walter Van Kleeck.

RECEIVING COMMITTEE:

Cornelius Van Wyck,   John R. Sleight,   Edward Burgess.

ON MERCHANDISE.

Henry W. Morris,   James G. Wood,   Robert W. Frost,
        Robert Slee,   John G. Boyd.

ON DECORATIONS.

Dr. E. H. Parker,   Mr. Wood,
" E. L. Beadle,   Mr. C. Franklin.

FLOOR COMMITTEE:

M. Vassar, jr.,   Jas. H. Weeks,   Peter B. Hayt,
Isaac W. White,   Robert Sanford,   John W. Davies,
E. M. Van Kleeck,   Prof. Wells,   Frank Stevens,
John R. Lent,   Geo. H. Beattys,   John H. Matthews,
Geo. P. Pelton,   Henry S. Frost,   Chas. Arnold,
        John A. Storm, Stormville.

DUTCHESS COUNTY ROOM.

Mrs. D. S. Jones,   Miss Varick,   Mrs. Franklin,
Mrs. C. H. Ruggles,   Mr. and Mrs. B. J. Lossing,   Miss Fanning,
Mrs. Buck,   Mrs. L. M. Arnold,   Miss DeGroff,
        Miss Henrietta Livingston.

SKATING POND.
Moses S. Beach.

PICTURE GALLERY.
Robert Sanford and Mr. Hoffer.

AGRICULTURE.
Geo. P. Pelton

FLORAL TEMPLE.

Mrs. Thos. L. Davies,   Miss E. Crosby,   Miss Broom,   Miss Swift,
        Miss Beadle,   Miss Fonda,   Miss Patton,
.

ON FLOWERS.

Mrs. John Thompson,   Mrs. D. S. Jones,   Mrs. Emott,
Mrs. C. H. Ruggles,   Mrs. T. L. Davies.

ON SANITARY HALL.

Mrs. Burnap,   Mrs. Winslow,
Mrs. Swift,   Mrs. Van Valkenburgh.

RECEIVING COMMITTEE, 361 MAIN ST.

Mrs. Patton,   Miss J. Varick,   Mrs. Geo. Wilkinson,
Miss Babcock,   " Mary Merritt,   " O. Fowler,
" Phinney   Mrs. Burnap,   " J. Parish,
Mrs. R. North,   Mrs. Mark Wilbur,   Mrs. H. Swift,
Mrs. Theodore Trivett, Miss Julia Crosby,   Mrs. Ellsworth.

RECEIVING COMMITTEE, SANITARY HALL.

Mrs. Geo. Wilkinson,   Mrs. Platt,   Mrs. Schram,   Mrs. H. D. Myers,
        Mrs. Henry Swift,   Mrs. Van Auden,   Mrs. Jacob Parish,

POST OFFICE.

Mrs. Joseph Wright,   Miss C. Allen,   Miss Rowe,
        Miss Shaw,   Miss Southwick.

APPROPRIATING COMMITTEE, REFRESHMENT DEPARTMENT.

Mrs. Burnap,   Mrs. LeGrand Dodge,   Mrs. E. Storm,
" G. B. Lent,   " Ab'm Wright,   " Major Patten,
" J. Parker,   Miss Merritt,   " Costar,
Mrs. Weddle,   Mrs. North.

APPRAISING AND APPROPRIATING COMMITTEE, FANCY DEPARTMENT.

Mrs. Capt. Coggswell,   Mrs. DeGroff,   Mrs. Jas. Reynolds,
" G. T. Brown,   " J. F. Hull,   " Boardman.
" R. James,   " Wm. S. Wright,

GIPSY TENT.

Mrs. Dr. Hoffman,   Mr. Costar,   Miss C. Van Wyck,
Miss S. Wilkinson,   Miss C. Beadle.

SWISS BOOTH.

Mrs Edward Beach,   Miss Julia Van Kleeck,   Miss Louisa Beach,
Miss Carrie Van Kleeck,   Miss Ellen Varick.

MILITARY TENT.

Mrs. Theodore Van Kleeck,   Mrs. Prof. Eastman,   Miss Belle Cornwell,
Miss Kate Cornwell,   Miss Booth,   " Mina North.

TELEGRAPH.

Mr. George Hill, United States Telegraph line.
" John E. Smith, of Eastman's College.

MUSIC.

Poughkeepsie Cornet Band.   Eastman's College Band.

OLD WOMAN IN HER SHOE.

Miss Julia Crosby,   Miss Netta Cary,
" Hasbrouck,   " Fannie Hageman.

PERFUMERY STAND.

Mrs. Col. Bailey,   Miss Mary Adams.

COTTAGE HILL TABLE.

Mrs. Rider,   Miss Mann,   Miss Paige.

POUGHKEEPSIE FANCY TABLE.

Mrs. Beadle,   Miss Sarah Varick,   Miss Carrie Sherman,
Miss Julia Jones,   Mrs. Geo. Innis,   " Mary Sterling,
Miss Alida Varick,   Miss Lizzie Wright.

POUGHKEEPSIE FANCY TABLE.

Mrs. Van Valkenburgh,   Miss Mary Johnson,   Miss Pauline Aweng,
Miss Maggie Crook,   Mrs. Morgan,   " M. Farnum,
Miss Mary Parker,   Miss Lizzie Parker.

FISHKILL TABLE.

Mrs. Wm. Verplank,   Miss Tilly Bois,   Miss Neilson,
" Kent,   " Crosby,   Mrs. J. Howland,
" E. P. Dickie,   " Verplank,   Miss Rumsey.

PHILADELPHIA TABLE.

Mrs. General Smith.

DOVER TABLE.

Mrs. Z. Rudd,   Mrs. A. Wright,
Miss Preston,   Miss Vincent.

POUGHKEEPSIE.

Mrs. Wood,   Miss Sarah Smith,   Miss G. Thomas,
Miss Louisa Ver Valin,   Mrs. Cornwell,   " E. Thomas,
Miss Susan Hughson,   Miss Ann Warring.

STANFORD TABLE.

Mrs. Holman.   Mrs. I. G. Sands.

INDEFATIGABLES.

Mrs. G. T. Brown,   Miss M. Reynolds,   Mrs. Fredricks,
" Dr. Dabois,   " F. Clark,   Miss Allie Lent,
Miss Martha Reynolds,   " L. Smith,   " E. Collingwood,
" Sarah Harris,   " Julia Freer,   " J. Clark,
" H. M. Southwick,   Mrs. Jas. Reynolds,   " J. Collingwood.
Miss M. Reynolds,   Miss Currier.

PAWLING.

Mrs. William Tabor,	Miss S. Kirby,	Miss Coffin,
Miss Fanny Kirby,	" A. Aiken,	" Sarah Wing.

WASHINGTON.

Mrs. Geo. B. Collin,	Miss Hattie Collin,	Miss Lucy Coffin.

POUGHKEEPSIE.

Mrs. Raub,	Miss Hattie Osborne,	Mrs. A. Wright.
" Ward,	" E. Candee,	Miss E. Fanning,
Miss R. Fanning,	" R. Gale,	" Alice Blanchard,
" Bell Fanning,	Mrs. Dobbs,	" K. Kettell,
	Miss Mary Dobbs.	

POUGHKEEPSIE.

Mrs. Booth,	Mrs. Tooker,
Miss Charlotte Wickes,	Miss Charlotte Davies,
" Hattie Thompson,	Mrs. Chas. Williams,
" A. Boardman,	Miss M. Swift.

HACKENSACK TABLE.

Mrs. Diddle,	Miss Jones,	The Misses Knapp,

REFRESHMENT DEPARTMENT, POUGHKEEPSIE TABLE.

Mrs. Matthews,	Miss Laura Emott,
" Dr. Fowler,	Mrs. D. R. Thompson,
Miss Mary Varick,	" Sarah Palmer,
" Kate V. S. Varick,	Miss Maggie Varick,
" Annie M. R. Varick,	" Jennie Van Kleeck,
" Jennie E. Varick,	" Gertrude Matthews,
" L. Humphrey,	" H. Humphrey,
	Mrs. O. Fowler.

POUGHKEEPSIE.

Mrs. A. Innis,	Mrs. Eastman,
" Dr. Hasbrouck,	" M. Wilber,
Miss H. Van Kleeck,	Miss Irene Beach,
" F. Clark,	" Martha Beardsley,
" Eliza Frost,	" Sarah Wright,
" A. K. Carpenter,	" Emma Bowne,
" Louisa Eldridge,	" Kate Shaw.
" Julia Frost,	

POUGHKEEPSIE.

Mrs. H. Shaw,	Mrs. Loyd,	Mrs. H. W. Morris,
" E. Van Kleeck,		Miss Annie Nelson,
Miss Lizzie Cramer,		" Mary Harris,
" Mary Bartlett,		" Eliza Wright,
" Sarah Bowne,		" Louisa Bartlett,
" Ella Taylor,		" Adele Dubois,
" R. Martin,		" Emily Morris.

BEEKMAN TABLE.

Miss Mary Noxon,	Miss Alma Sterling,
Mrs. Benjamin S. Broas,	" Sheldon,
Miss Brock,	" Graham,
" Woodell,	" Clapp.

LAGRANGE TABLE.

Mrs. Simmons,	Miss Clapp,	Mrs. Hurd,
" Ayrault,	" Pells,	" Haviland,
" Van Benschoten,	" Hart,	Miss Downing,
	Miss Sherman,	Miss Able.

EAST FISHKILL TABLE.

Miss Adriance,	Miss Bartow,	Miss Bartow,
Miss D. Horton,		Mrs. Brinckerhoff.

POUGHKEEPSIE.

Mrs. John Trowbridge,
" N. C. Trowbridge,
Miss Sophia Wilkinson,
" Eliza Wilkinson,
" Eliza C. Trowbridge,
" Millie Coffin,
" Maria Booth,

Mrs. John Grant,
" George Vail,
Miss M. Trowbridge,
" E. Trowbridge,
" C. Allen,
" R. North,
" M. Palmatier.

RESTAURANT.

Mrs. Brackett,
" E. Cary,
" Wright,
" Cornell,
" Dr. Jillson,
" Bartlett,
Miss Babcock,
" Van Wyck,
" M. E. Storm,
" Julia Varick,
" Coffin,
" M. Everett,
" Brewer,
" M. Thorn,

Mrs. Hagar,
" J. Sterling,
" A. D. Cole,
" Lawrence,
" Martin,
Miss C. Thomas,
" Mary Wilson,
" Hasbrouck,
" E. Coffin,
" C. Trivett,
" M. Flint,
" E. Barnes,
" Knapp,
" Hattie Degroff,

Miss M. Wilson,

CIRCULAR.

—o—

A Fair is to be held in the City of Poughkeepsie, on the 15th March, 1864, for the relief of the Sick and Wounded Soldiers of our National Army.

It is designed to be a Fair on a large scale. Every branch of Agriculture, Trade, Industry and Art will be invited to contribute to it. We call on the farmers of the rich county of Dutchess to send in the products of their fields and dairies. We ask our factories, workshops, mills, every branch of trade, for a specimen of the best thing they can turn out.

We call on all our loyal women for the exercise of their taste and industry.

Every one who can produce anything that has money value will give a sample of his work as an offering to the cause of National Unity.

Clergymen of all denominations are earnestly requested to interest their parishes in this enterprise. The press is requested to give it wide circulation and earnest encouragement. You are invited personally to coöperate in it; if you cannot do so, give it the influence of your name or position. We rely on your aid, and call on all without hesitation to assist in this benevolent work of relieving the sufferings of our Sick and Wounded Soldiers, who have gone forth in our defense, and to whose noble efforts we shall be indebted, under God, for the preservation of our nationality. It should be remembered that the United States Sanitary Commission bestows its benefactions on the Sick and Wounded of our Army and Navy without regard to State, Rank or Color; hence it has claims on the liberality and labor of all loyal men and women.

Two Committees, one of ladies and one of gentlemen, have been appointed, and Managers in every town in the county have been appointed to carry out this undertaking. The ladies have engaged a room at 361 Main street, where the receiving committee will be in attendance to receive all contributions, whether loans or donations. For ladies from the country towns tables will be reserved, at which they can display and sell their productions of taste and industry. All donations will be sold at the Fair for cash, and the avails of such sales, together with all contributions in money, paid over to George T. Strong, Treasurer of the United States Sanitary Commission, at New York. Contributions are invited, for temporary loan and exhibition, of Pictures, Works of Art, Trophies, Battle Flags, Relics and Mementoes of the War; these will be arranged in a room devoted to that purpose.

Flowers and Floral Designs, Green-house Plants in pots, are solicited.

Supplies for the refreshment tables, Turkeys, Ducks, Chickens, Hams, Tongues, Birds, Game, Oysters,—all these (except the latter) should be carefully cooked.

Tea, Coffee, Chocolate, Sugar and Cream, Cakes, Pies, Preserves, Jellies, Jams and Fruits in Cans, Honey, Pickles, Vegetables of all Varieties, Apples, Butter.

At the close of the Fair a catalogue of articles contributed, with the names of donors, will be published.

Contributions, whether loans or donations, should be sent to the Committee Rooms, 361 Main street.

Contributions of money should be sent to Miss Sarah M. Carpenter, 389 Mill street. Treasurer.

MRS. CHARLES H. RUGGLES, Secretary.

HISTORY OF THE
Dutchess Co. and Poughkeepsie Sanitary Fair.

—o—

The brief space allotted to the fulfillment of this design, from its origin, early in February, to its complete and triumphant success in the middle of March, entitle it to a place in the history of events of our time.

So suddenly was it received into favor, apparently by all hearts, that it seemed the spontaneous growth of a soil already warmed by patriotism, and enriched with benevolence. There had been tongues eloquent in depicting the necessities of our wounded soldiers, and the deprivations of the sick. Gentle hands had labored for them, kind offerings had been made, and active spirits were on the alert to awaken in their behalf renewed interest and sympathy. At length the feeling which had for some time been kindling in many a breast spoke out in action. On Friday, February 5th, a meeting of ladies was called at the Gregory House, intended to include all interested in that happy organization, which, from the commencement, augured most favorable results.

The work immediately commenced in little auxiliary circles throughout the town. All amusements and recreations were, as far as possible, diverted towards this object. Young ladies plied their nimble fingers in crochet work, and other delicate fabrications. Gentlemen contributed towards the expense of materials, and gave their countenance to the project.

Six weeks only were allotted to the completion of the whole design. Many shook their heads, and thought the time too short; but the officers never wavered. The Secretary immediately issued her circulars. Stirring, trumpet-toned words called upon all the good and noble throughout the county to unite with this city in one broad manifestation of generous feeling towards those in arms for our defense. Managers were appointed in every town, receiving their commissions from the Secretary, and cordial invitations to coöperate in the work so well begun. Daily Executive meetings were held, and weekly public ones succeeded. A gentlemen's Advisory Committee was selected to aid in business transactions. The building intended for the Fair was soon chosen a large unoccupied Coach Factory on Main street being magnanimously offered, free of expense, by the owner, Matthew Vassar, Esq., and gratefully accepted by the Executive Committee.

The fitting up of the building by able hands immediately commenced. A chaotic scene at first ensued. Speedily order and comeliness were evolved, out of rough and unshapely materials. The gigantic work, so rapid in its progress, ordained by sovereign female will, reminded one of the famous ice palace commanded so hastily into being by the great Russian Empress in the days of Autocratic power. As surely as speedily as that, this fabric of ours assumed shape of beauty and form of strength, though not "silently as a dream;" for here were sounds of busy labor and dust of disturbed elements; but all asserted the power of female sovereignty, and the willing deference of manly courtesy which in highest civilization yields to woman highest homage.

Meanwhile, the inner structure, the mental organization of Committees and sub-Committees was unremittingly carried on, at the rooms 361 Main street. Already donations began to flow in. At the first meeting Mrs.

B. J. Lossing commenced the subscription list by her own name for $50; others as generously followed. Bad roads and worse weather dampened somewhat the enthusiasm which had been expected from the inhabitants of our eastern hills and plains; but some did answer nobly to the call, and few were entirely indifferent. We cannot help feeling, if a little of the same genius and energy which awakened a whole county to action, upon this occasion, were exercised upon the broad field subject to our National Councils—if there were the same true steel, the same good ring of metal, among our Generals—some quick blow might be struck, some sudden assault made, rendering less needful this female guard for hospital aid at home.

Preparations went on vigorously through the town. Schools gave Concerts, Soirees and Tableaux, bringing in large donations to the treasury. Ladies engaged popular lecturers at their own expense, the proceeds to be given entirely to the same object. Where so many did well it would be invidious to particularize. The ladies who gave their time, means and energies to the work needed no incentive of popular applause to induce them to such efforts. Actuated by the lofty spirit of patriotism, upheld by the blessed reward of doing good, their motives required no oblation of mere human praise. There were some holding conspicuous positions and giving large donations, whose wisdom and benevolence could not but be appreciated by the public. Others worked in secret, and gave according to their means, more liberally, perhaps, than those who contributed so nobly from their wealth and abundance. Without these little unnoticed rills small would have been the mighty stream.

OPENING OF THE FAIR.

The auspicious day at length arrived—the morning of the 15th of March. Preparations were complete. The faithless became believing, the wavering confirmed; for, precisely at 1 o'clock, doors were opened, and all was ready. Following the long line of carriages in the street, and the throng of pedestrians on the sidewalk, a stranger, without inquiry, would readily have found the road to Sanitary Hall. The building, without, was not over-fair to view, although the gay flags gave tokens of promise; but within,

> "'Twas glittering all and light,
> A thronging scene of figures bright,
> It glowed upon our dazzled sight,"

even as the sudden glare of king and courtiers shone upon the astonished vision of the fair " Lady of the Lake." In truth, the general aspect of the building was like a beautiful picture out of dreamland. There was such abundance of evergreens, in all imaginable places, as never grew inside of brick walls before: then there were pictures, curtains, mirrors and flags innumerable; sufficient in themselves, with stars, stripes and eagles, to have made a very respectable "Fourth of July Oration." Tables on the first floor were loaded with every viand that was goodly to the eye or pleasant to the taste, while above, on the fancy floor, such a tasteful collection of *beautiful*, *charming* and *elegant* objects met the view; such *loves of mats*, such *perfect tidies*, such *darlings* of *pincushions*, as never bewildered the senses of man before, especially in the good town of Poughkeepsie; and more than all, both up-stairs and down-stairs, such bright eyes and pink cheeks, and real Grecian heads, surmounted with the daintiest little caps, were seen gliding in and out of booths and floral bowers, and from behind tables, beguiling poor, innocent, unprotected young men out of dollars and dimes, with such fascinating grace—giving the color of a blush to a cigar case, or the flavor of a smile to an oyster stew, in such a guileless way that the highwayman's time-honored demand, "your money or your life," was small persuasion compared with theirs. When woman "stoops to conquer" she is always victorious. Upon this great general principle, laid deep in the hearts of our race, rests the success of all Sanitary Fairs.

And so to descend, or rather ascend, to particularize. It will be necessary, in order to sound the heights and depths of this great subject, to commence at the third story and recount all the marvels to be seen from this eminent beginning downward. First, then, the upper story was preëminently attic. Here culminated the Æsthetic aspirations of the Committee; for here was to be seen the picture gallery, exhibited without charge, thus permitting the fine arts to be accessible to all. It must be acknowledged, the collection was small. Time had not permitted any of those great works which might have been undertaken under other circumstances, and which there was plenty of genius in the community to have accomplished. Here let us pause, to admire the wisdom which allowed such brief space for preparation. As the great fire at Wolf's Craig gave to its faithful servitor a potential and unvarying excuse for the absence of silver plate, damask hangings, and all other valuable furniture usually belonging to the abode of a wealthy nobleman, so we, availing ourselves of a similar apology, once for all will say that, whatever defects may be noticed in this Fair, whatever omissions there may be in the way of grandeur and display, making it in the least to differ from the great Boston and Brooklyn Fairs, is entirely owing to want of time. Thus with the picture gallery: a little of the mellowing of time would have improved it. Nevertheless, there were some very pretty pictures on exhibition and for sale. One of Peter, the hermit, finished with great care and study, and a fine appreciation of her subject, by a young lady of this city, elicited many high compliments, and was well deserving of them all. Two very pretty little country scenes, by a young lady of America, were presented to the Fair, and sold quickly. Other ladies presented creditable productions, among which perhaps the most coveted was a delicious bunch of white grapes. Mr. Sandford is the able Superintendent of this department.

The Museum appears next. Here are some valuable Indian relics, autographs, and other curiosities. For the famous skating pond and a curious apparatus for making old women young again the ladies are indebted to M. S. Beach, Esq. These attract numerous visitors, and appeal especially to the juvenile taste. On the opposite side of the gallery a huge brass knocker, with portentous sound, announces visitors to

THE OLD DUTCHESS COUNTY ROOM.

As the Committee owe this great attraction of the upper floor chiefly to the joint labors of Mr. B. J. Lossing and M. Vassar, jr., a more detailed account of room and furniture will be given by one of the gentlemen most active in its construction. As to the old families, the Van Tassels, the Van Deusens, the Vanderhuydens, which held high festival here during the Fair, they have gone back into their portrait galleries and haunted chambers, from which they emerged in quaint and antique costume, for a little season, to witness the indolent habits, the free and easy manners, the absence of witchcraft and other degeneracies of our time.

Leaving the Duchess room, we run counter to a series of mowing machines and other formidable tokens of a mechanical age, relieved by a little pastoral touch in the shape of a huge Southdown sheep. Mr. Geo. Pelton earns laurels here by his successful disposal of farming implements and wooden ware. "The *great moral show*" of the live Alligator and the

Barber's Shop are also successfully cried up, on this floor, by Mr. Charles Arnold, with a zeal which would do credit to the owner of a whole menagerie.

Descending to the Fancy Hall, directly in front of us, is

THE SWISS BOOTH,

whose complete furniture of jewelry and other adornments, with the exception of one Afghan, was the munificent donation of the President, Mrs. James Winslow. In this booth, is to be seen and heard, the famous Bullfinch, the smallest singing bird known, which starts out from its tiny cage at an instant's warning, sings two cheery little songs, as though glad to greet the light, then springs back to its prison, and is seen no more, till the hour comes around.

Crossing the Hall, we reach

THE POST OFFICE,

under the able superintendence of Mrs. Joseph Wright. The Postmistress has certainly a laborious post, inasmuch as she must provide lovers and love-letters for those who have none, furnish good news whenever it is called for, and labor with hand and brain when others rest.

Now appears the long array of fancy tables, broken in upon by the classic portal of

THE FLORAL TEMPLE,

whose graceful columns, wreathed with evergreens, and cool marble tables, laden with flowers, do honor to the ladies originating the design. Mrs. Thomas L. Davies and Mrs. James Emott preside over the temple offerings, while six fair young priestesses waft incense from flowers as the crowd passes by.

Following the line of fancy tables, seven are noted as belonging to the "*City of Poughkeepsie*," one of them bearing the name of "Cottage Hill Seminary." The whole seven are so elegantly furnished, and superbly decorated, each having some peculiar attraction of its own, that it would be impossible to bestow distinctive commendation. Crowds of friends and patrons thronged around them all. Familiar faces appeared beside every counter. Goods were so tempting, and displayed with such tact, and good will, that if we had not emptied our purse to the first cashier encountered, that little transaction would certainly have been accomplished to the second, and so on around the Hall. We are proud of our City tables. Ladies have labored diligently to adorn them with every style of fancy work accessible to skill and application. The finer productions of art are also upon them. Flowers whose colors will not fade. Faces that change not by time. And the cheerful countenances everywhere met, show that these are truly offerings of the heart to a most worthy cause.

Here, too, are our kind and faithful allies, the country towns, bringing their treasures from afar. Conspicuous by position, and dazzling in its array of brilliant goods, welcome to the name of

FISHKILL.

Well do we know those fertile vales, those wood-crowned hills, and the rugged rocks upon the mountain side. The very soil to bind its children to it with strongest love; and here with patriotic zeal, we find them, earnestly aiding our common country, and our suffering brethren.

DOVER.

She, too, is here, from the region of the Stone Church and of magnificent mountain gorges. Her quiet secluded plains, have given time for meditation, and the result is a literary development, for this table abounds in books.

NEW HACKENSACK,

a near neighbor, has shown good neighborly interest, by rendering substantial aid to the cause, in which all are laboring. A hearty welcome, and kind greetings to all as we pass on.

STANFORD,

a name which thrills us with memories of old days, of a home upon the hills and distant mountain summits golden in the sunset, stands meekly over a small table on our left. Having but one week's notice, she too is here.

WASHINGTON AND PAWLING,

two other great agricultural towns, rich in flocks and herds, and friendly inhabitants, last but not least on our list, they too are here, bringing rich goods and pleasant faces, to complete the circuit of the fancy floor.

THE MILITARY BOOTH,

in the centre of the hall, is very attractive to gentlemen, because of the startling costume of its ladies, and the peculiarly gentlemanly wares, of which they dispose :—Tobacco, Cigars, Smoking Caps, and the like.

THE GIPSY TENT

denotes its profound wisdom, and knowledge of the future, by a significant owl over the entrance. This tent is only occupied at evening. We used to believe, that gipsies prowled about at night, for food and gains, but loanged in their dwellings through the day. We are glad to see that his august majesty, King Coster the first, of Egyptian lineage, and Pharonic dynasty, clad in his most regal garb, gathered from six quarters of the globe, has adopted the domestic habit of spending his evenings at home.

Suddenly the atmosphere seems laden with sweetness. We turn and find ourselves in front of a small *perfumery stand*, tended by a pretty lady, who appears to be doing a marvelous business.

The little old woman who lives in a shoe is the presiding genius of this part of the hall. Her dolls diminish rapidly, and she handles spectacles and snuff box to the admiration of beholders.

Descending, another flight of broad steps, we land in the midst of

THE REFRESHMENT FLOOR.

This is under the especial superintendence of Mrs. Burnap, whose task of arrangement has been laborious, and whose duties still continue to be arduous, inasmuch as she is constantly presiding at the head of a mighty feast. On this floor are four Poughkeepsie, and three country tables, East Fishkill, LaGrange and Beekman. Decorations, evergreens, flags and pictures make all the tables attractive and pleasing. Of the Poughkeepsie tables two are devoted to Oysters, Coffee and other substantial food ; the remaining two are laden with Ice Cream, Cakes and Confectionary. Of course the latter admit more ornament, and are crowned with aspiring pyramids. The Eagle's Nest seems enterprising and original, and its motto, *Pro Bono Militum* shows that " we have not forgotten our Latin."

Country boards are crowded with friends, whose appetites seem conveniently renewed every hour or two, for the sake of patronizing home production. Indeed our own citizens are often found forsaking their allegiance, and sitting down to a feast spread by some alluring damsel on the east side of the hall.

The Treasurer's desk is situated near the stairway. Miss Carpenter, with her whole heart in the success of the Fair, sits here from the opening to the closing of the Ticket Office, performing the pleasant duty of

14

receiving donations, checks and greenbacks, depositing the same in the Sanitary Treasury. With able assistants, she has the entire superintendence of the monetary concerns of the Fair.

The all important receiving room and the busy, bustling kitchen each occupy a share of this floor.

THE RESTAURANT

next claims our attention. This, as is customary, occupies the basement. Warm dinners are to be served here from 2 until 9 every day. Many ladies of this city are busily engaged in preparations. The office of waiting maid at these tables is no sinecure; but there are many here able to dignify with grace and beauty even the unadorned region of the Restaurant. A party of Bank Directors are to dine at 4. It is to be hoped that their hearts will be so opened by the good cheer as to draw liberal checks upon their own banks when they ascend.

We have glanced through the building on this its opening day. The admission fee is fifty cents, and the house is full. Many season tickets have been sold.

WEDNESDAY.—Rev. H. W. Beecher lectured last evening for the benefit of the Sanitary Fair. The whole expense was paid by Mr. Jas. Winslow, and the entire proceeds, $300, have been placed in the Treasury. A thronging multitude is here to day. Abundant sales are made. The tables begin to abate in splendor. By evening the crowd is so dense that fears are entertained for the safety of the building. But the good walls stand firm, although the sale of tickets is for a time prudently suspended. This second evening the assets amount to $9,500, and the Fair is voted a success.

THURSDAY.—The crowd is somewhat diminished. It is possible to move about without danger of being crushed. A little sensation is made by a visit from the Sunday School of the Congregational Church. The children form in front of the Treasurer's desk; Mr. Corning makes a neat little speech, and $150 is deposited as the Sunday School gift.

FRIDAY.—Still a busy multitude at Sanitary Hall. Tables begin to look faded. Sales continue at reduced prices. The Fair received a visit to day from the children of the Home. Eastman's band continues to discourse music as often as could be expected.

SATURDAY.—By the wise counsels of the managers, goods left on hand are marked so low as to ensure a sale, and prevent the greater sacrifice of an auction. This is the last day. Ladies from the country leave their vacant tables and return home. The Restaurant coalesces with the refreshment floor. At evening a fishing pond receives the remaining fancy articles, and fishing commences. Great merriment follows—two shillings a fish—every one catches something on his hook. By 9 o'clock nearly all is sold. Nothing left for an auction, except two or three pictures, some frozen flowers in pots, an order for coal, and the lumber used in the building. The Fair closes with more than $18,000 in the Treasury.

Now the busy scene is over. The joyful and triumphant occasion has passed by. As we look back upon it, with hearts full of gratitude, some expression of thanks seems due to those who labored so zealously from the beginning towards the success of this worthy object. Thanks! abundant thanks! to the lady officers of the Fair; who devoted their time, influence and means to the undertaking. Thanks to the gentlemen who, in their several committees, fulfilled so well the arduous tasks they so willingly assumed. It is the pleasant task of the historian to commemorate noble deeds. Noble was the self-sacrifice of those ladies who stepped a century backward, to the good old time of female heroism and manly daring, to give this generation a living picture of the past. If not the dust, the smoke of a century was certainly around them; and the dignified grace, which received alike visitors of all ranks and ages, would have done honor to the day when those rich brocades shone, perhaps, amid the stately courtesy of a colonial court, or in the purer atmoshere of our own early republican era. Surely spinning wheel was never so attractive before, nor olycokes displayed to more admiring eyes. Thanks to those ladies and gentlemen who so cordially aided in their little drama of history.

Honor to the ladies and gentlemen who labored so faithfully in the decoration of the fancy floor. The taste and elegance which have adorned many a private salon were here brought forward, for the public good and at the call of charity. Conservatories and greenhouses were rifled of their spring glories, to furnish the daily demands of the Floral Temple, and nearly every country seat from Rhinebeck to Fishkill joined in the tribute. Ladies who seldom left the sanctuary of home were here seen doing honor to the place and breathing their natural atmosphere of flowers. Thanks to them, and to all, the fair matrons and gentle girls, who stood among their tempting booths and bowers, to barter the work of their own hands, for the meed of well doing.

And, as the lowlier should be more exalted, *higher praise* to the denizens of the first floor, who stood ready to minister to the weary, faint and hungry. The delicate waiting maids, watching with painstaking care beside the little tables, contributed no small share to the abundant proceeds of the refreshment floor. Doubtless many a *young* gentleman became intoxicated over his coffee, and fell to dreaming of a home of his own with such a fairy to guard it.

Last in the descent, but more praiseworthy still, were the ladies of the Restaurant. No fanciful adornings nor beautiful surroundings cast a fairy glamor upon their labors. *Real* and *arduous service* fell to the lot of those who condescended to these tasks, willingly performing their duties, in order that all might be well fulfilled. *Thanks to them, and to all, ladies and gentlemen, at home and abroad*, who sacrificed their time and their substance, in turn to all departments, and liberally aided in the success of all.

Thanks to the gardeners and nurserymen, who generously answered the calls made upon them, and gave of their productions for the benefit of the Fair. Thanks to the mechanics, artisans, merchants and tradesmen, who contributed of their labors and goods, or assisted gratuitously in the preparation of Sanitary Hall. All have done well.

This Sanitary Fair has been the spontaneous offering of Duchess County. And when we see what she can do with such brief notice, and amid such disadvantages of season, what may we not expect if the time ever come when greater deeds and nobler sacrifices shall be demanded at her hands? The home of our fathers—the seat of colonial wisdom during the revolutionary struggle, the venerable mother of noble sons and daughters--we believe in her truth and patriotism, we rejoice in her munificent liberality. Thanks for her aid in this benevolent effort. Thanks, above all, to a kind Providence! which tempered the rough winds of March to mildness, and preserved the lives and health of all concerned. May kind and generous thoughts follow to their homes those who met with us last week, and may the charity which looketh pleasantly upon all things bring its sweetness to their hearts, so that every memory of this great festival shall be one of love, and every thought a blessing.

TREASURER'S REPORT.

RECEIPTS.

Beekman Refresh't Table, &c.,$	394 50
Dover Fancy Table,	258 35
East Fishkill Refresh't Table,	134 20
Fishkill Fancy Table,	702 53
Fishkill Land. Cash Donations,	106 00
Wap's Falls, Mrs. J. Faulkner,	139 00
New Hackensack Soc. & Table,	214 34
LaGrange Refreshment Table,	514 40
Milan, by Mrs. O. Booth,	15 00
Pawling Table & Cash Donat's,	328 49
Pine Plains, " "	192 45
Red Hook, " "	480 60
Rhinebeck, " "	108 00
Stanford Table & " "	65 08
Union Vale, " "	20 00
Philadelphia Table,	102 68
Sale of Tickets,	2,336 64
Skating Pond,	421 09
Post Office,	113 91
Agricultural Department,	837 45
Schools,	917 00
Tickets and Sales of Old Room,	536 14
Sales of Pictures, Cloths, &c.,	549 41
Wash'n Table & Cash Donat's,	203 80
Cloak Room,	43 63
Swiss Booth,	489 72
Military Tent,	256 67
Floral Temple,	411 57
Old Woman in her Shoe,	91 58
Grab-bag, Barber Shop and Gipsy Tent,	55 11
Telegraph Office, Floral Cake,	23 75
Fish Pond,	38 30
Po'keepsie Fancy Department,	2,750 66
" Refreshment "	1,188 99
Lower Restaurant,	534 23
Cash Donat's, Po'keepsie, &c.,	2,996 60
Table, no name or number,	69 00
	$18,640 87

EXPENDITURES.

Paid Mr. Wood, Architect, $	100 00
Expense of Old Room,	85 24
" Post Office,	9 15
Nelson Seaman's Bill,	88 10
Heath & Cramer's "	120 00
Smith & Son's, "	553 87
Mr. Johnson's "	345 00
Gas Bill and for Laying Pipe,	15 95
Rent of Committee Room,	15 00
Mr. Dean's Bill,	63 17
Disc't & Counterfeit Money,	38 55
Paid Watchmen,	46 50
" Workwomen,	116 48
" for Cartage—not inclu'd in other bills,	12 77
Stationery,	27 79
Paid Workmen,	95 25
Groceries,	138 21
Lumber,	102 93
Printing,	82 82
Small bills paid,	282 39
Tickets,	19 00
Money in Bank,	16,282 72
	$18,640 87

A few donations are yet to be collected and turned into money, and there are some small claims for which bills have not yet been presented. A final report will be made as soon as practicable.

SARAH M. CARPENTER,
Treasurer.

Examined by the Committee April 13, 1864, and found correct.

Whole am't of Money rec'd, $18,640 87
" " " exp'd, 2,358 15

Balance in Treasury, $16,282 72
F. W. DAVIS,
HENRY S. FROST, }Com.
JOHN H. MATHEWS.

CASH DONATIONS INCLUDED IN THE TREASURER'S REPORT

From Poughkeepsie, &c.

Mrs Benson J Lossing	$ 50
Mrs Nathan Sanford	25
Mrs George Innis	50
Miss Wyeth	20
Mrs Dr Beadle	25
Mrs Morgan Carpenter	25
Mr John F Winslow, Troy,	50
Mrs Hooker	25
Mrs James Emott	25
Prof Morse	50
G Van Kleeck & Co by J G Boyd	50
Mrs Wm Davies	50
Mrs Wm A Davies	50
Mrs Jacob Parrish	25
Mrs Mary Van Wagenen	20
Mrs Atwill	20
Mr Charles Crooke	30
J G Boyd as Treas of Mer Com	91 30
Mrs Clinton Jones	20
Mr John A Roosevelt	25
Mrs Oscar Fowler	20
Miss Rita Van Valkenburgh	5
Mrs C H Raggles	50
Judge Ruggles	50
Mrs Henry Rose, Yates County,	20
Mrs Henry Swift	15
Mrs Henry H Stevens	20
Messrs Seward & Hayt	25
Dr Hasbrouck	19
Mrs Alson Ward	2
Lieut R L Burnett	10
Mr Jacob B Jewett	20
Gen T L Davies	50
Dr Roberts	5
Mr Wilson B Sheldon	2
Dr Robert Gill	25
Mrs Daniel S Miller, Hyde Park,	50
Mrs Christopher Smith, Staatsb,	10
Mr J F S teaf	200
Mr D T Sparks	3
Mr L P Shear, New York,	30
Mr Charles Eastmead	15
Mr James Smith jr	20
Mr Levi Arnold	5
Mr D C Foster	10
Mr E B Osborne	5
Messrs Platt & Schram	19 22
Mr Wm Bennet, florist,	5
Mrs Hughson	5
Mrs H Jewett	3
Mrs Rosekrans	2
Mrs J Underhill	1
Mr James Winslow	350 27
Mr Wm Barton	5
Mr Jas Caldwell, Philadelphia,	5
Soldiers' Aid Soc, Patterson, Putnam Co, by Mrs Reed F Akin,	15
Mr Moses S Beach	56 64
Collected by Mr Pelton (see list)	805
Collected by A Varick (see list)	265
Mr Wm Simmons	7 69
S V Frost & Son	15 50
Heath & Cramer	20
Mr Henry Pierce	5
Collingwood & Son	5
Mr J H Warner	25

Collecte'd by Mr. G. P. Pelton,

Mr Matthew Vassar	$ 50
Mr Matthew Vassar jr	50
C M & G P Pelton (1 case pins)	50
Mr Joseph Smart	10
Mr H G Eastman	25
Mr S M Buckingham	50
Mr Warren Skinner	20
Mr L Elting	10
Mr S V Frost	5
Mr Henry Van Wart jr	10
A Friend	10
Mr LeGrand Dodge	10
Mr Wm S Wright	25
Mr E Bech	50
Mr F H Newbold	50
Gifford, Sherman & Innis	200
Mr I C Doughty	10
Mr William H Crosby	5
Mr Richard J Van Nostran (calf)	5
Mr Moses S Beach	25
Mr Wm A Davies	100
Mr C W Swift	50
Mr John S Sleight	10

Collected by Mr. A. Varick.

Mr W C Sterling	25
Mr John B Sherman	25
Prof Brown	10
Mr F W G Jones	10
Mr T Lawrence	10
Mr Walter Corlies	10
Mr George Corlies	10
Mr T Brinkerhoff	2
Mr R Pudney	2
Mr W McGeorge	2
Mr E Everitt	2
Mr R N Palmer	3
Mr J T Baker	2
Mr C B Jenkins	2
Mr A Adams	2
Dr R A Varick	10
Mr Edgar Van Kleeck	10
Dr P Barnes	3
Mr L B Sacket	2
Mr C S Van Wyck	2
Cash	1
Mr G C Burnap	25
Mr Abraham Varick	10
Mr J Emott	10
Mr A'son Ward	10
Mr William Barnes	10
Mr A J Courrier	5
Mr D H Barnes	5
Mr S C Abeel	5
Mr R C Meeks	5
Mr J P H Tallman	5
Mr E Q Eldridge	5
Mr James H Weeks	5
Mr J O Hoffman	5
Dr Bolton	5
Dr Hoffman	5
Mr W Bradley	3
Dr Richards	2

Schools.

Congregational Sabbath School,	150
Poughkeepsie Female Collegiate School, Rev C D Rice Princi l,	85

18

Poughkeepsie Female Academy,
 Rev D G Wright Principal, $354
Cottage Hill Seminary, Rev G T
 Rider Principal, 172
Collegiate School, O Bisbee Prin 50
Military Institute, Mr Warring, 106

Pine Plains.

Rev Wm Sayre, from Pres Chur, 50
Ladies of Pine Plains, by Mrs
 Wooden and Miss Wilson 142 45

Cash Donations from town of Beekman.

Mrs Thomas Brill	1
Mr H B Mead	2
Mr Alfred Noxon	1
Mr Polaemus Humphrey	1

Collected by Miss Sterling and Miss Noxon for
Beekman Table.

Mr Gilbert B Noxon	10
Mr J Snelden	5
Mr J S Holmes	5
Mr Amos Denton	5
Mr Daniel L Noxon	1
Mr Egbert Wooden	1
Mr Wm E Haxtun	10
Mr Rily Mory	5
Mr George Fiagler	5
Mr Harvey Emigh	5
Mr Levi Reynolds	1
Mr Abraham Dutcher	2
Mr Alexander Bryant	3
Mr Egbert C Noxon	2
Mr Morgan S Washburn	2
Mr John H Williams	2
Mr J H Lee	1
Mr Joseph Morey	1
Mr S B Ackerman	2
Mr James N Ashley	5
Mr John Fiagler	3
Mr Wm H Seaman	3
Mr Wm Van Wyck	50
Mr John Cypher	2
Mr Philip H Knapp	3
Mr Elmore R Noxon	2
Mr Egbert Sweet	5
Mr Clark A Nickerson	2
Mr Wm H Wright	1
Mr Charles Humphrey	50
Mr Samuel C Vail	1
Mr Wm Dougity	5
Mr Weyman Dodge	5
Mr George Dean	1
Mr Henry P Woolley	4
Mr Henry C Bull	1
Mr Richard C Rogers	1
Mr Theodore Peters	1
Mr Charles Brill	1
Mr Charles Sherman	5
Mr Thomas Brill	1
Mr John Peters	1
Mr George B Foot	1
Mr George T Doughty	1
Mr Wm Flagler	1
Mr James E Dutcher	1
Mr Jarvis Noxon	2
Mr Joseph Doughty	1
Mr John H Cook	2

Mr N B Reynolds	$	1
Mr Benjamin H Sisson		2
Mr James C Sweet		3
Mr S V Rogers		2
Mr Henry Armstrong		1
Mr P A Skidmore		3
Mr Alex Baker		1
Mr Wm W Haxtun		5
Mr H D Sterling		2
Mrs S V Rogers		1
Miss Catharine Noxon		1
Mrs Levi Odell		1
Mrs Thomas Cypher		1
Mrs Amanda Hall		2 50
Mrs Ann Gregory		2 50
Mrs Henry C Bull		2
Mrs Caroline W Peters		1
Mrs Egbert Rogers		1
Mrs Wm C Carl		1
Mrs John Bull		1
Miss Carrie Brock		2
Mrs Theodore Peters		1
Mrs Caristopher Brow		7
Mrs Mary D Seaman		1
Mrs George B Foot		1
Mrs John Peters		2
Mrs Gilbert Flagler		1
Mrs Theodore Flagler		1
Mrs John W Hotch		1
Mrs Wm Flagler		1
Mrs James A Arthur		1
Mrs Abraham Sherman		1
Mrs S B Ackerman		1
Mrs Egbert Spencer		1
Mrs Philip F Knapp		1
Mrs Henry P Woolley		1
Mrs George Johnson		1
Mrs Myron H Sherman		50
Mrs Emily Vanderburgh		1
Mrs Wm W Haxtun		2
Mrs John B Velie		1
Mrs Levi Reynolds		2
Mrs J H Cook		2
Mrs S A Truet		1
Mrs Amos D Baker		1
Mrs Phebe Hewelling		50
Mrs Jane Billings		1
Mrs George Caldwell		1
Mrs B H Brinkerhoff		1
Mrs John Williams		1
Mrs H J Haviland		1
Mrs Joseph Morey		1
Mrs Leonard Hall		1
Mrs James Skidmore		1
Mrs Harvey Bryant		2
Miss Susan Emigh		1
Mrs Laban Rowe		1
Mrs Perry D Delamater		1
Mrs Morgan S Washburn		1
Miss Sarah A Barnes		50
Mrs John W Flagler		1
Miss Mary Flagler		1
Mrs Daniel Thomas		1
Mrs Charles Bull		1

Cash Contributions of town of La Grange
for LaGrange Table.

Mr George Ayrault	10
Mr Peter R Sleight	5

	$				$	
Mrs Peter R Sleight	8	5	Mr J R Needam	6	1	
Rachel Pells	2		Mr B Hopkins		1	
Rachel Velie		50	Mr V B Ackerman		1	
Annie Haviland	3		Mr J V B Stoutenburgh			75
Annie B Downing	3		Mr J V B Voorhees		3	
Sarah J Brown	2		Mrs H D Needam			17
Mr James Howard	5		A Friend		1	
Mrs Isaac Cornell	3		Mr P Dates		5	
Mr Elias Titus	10		Mr N Ganse		2	
Mr Silas Sweet	3		Messrs N & L Ostrander		3	
Mrs Wilson	1		Mr H D Platt		5	
Mrs J H Robinson	1		Mr P Myers	\	1	
Mr Peter B Clapp	3		Mr G Bishop		1	
Mr G W Clapp	3		Mr C Dearin		1	
Mr E Barlow	1		Mrs S Seward		2	
Mr John G Pells	2		Mrs E Dodge		1	
Mr C Boyd	3		Mrs Wm Seward		1	
Mr W H Hopkins	5		Mrs P M Ostrander		1	
David Barnes	5		Mrs Stephen Cornell		1	
Edward Flagler	3		Mrs S J Robinson		1	
Cornelius Miller	3		Miss Sarah Cornell		1	
Wm C Smith	1		Mrs H D Hayt		2	
Sebring Ackerman	1		Mrs M Mott		5	
Adrian Montort	2		Mrs Cornell		2	
James Townsend	10		Mrs S Sweet		2	
Rosanna Townsend	10		Mrs Forman		1	
Smith Upton	5		Mrs Van Amburgh		4	
George Potter	3		Mrs Kenson		5	
Mrs George Potter	1	50	Dr Underhill		1	
D W Odell	2		Mr J R Phillips		1	
Jacob Velie	2		Mr George Phillips		1	
Isaac J Clapp	10		Miss A Van Amburgh		1	
Richard Kenworthy	5		Mrs M Wood		2	
Mrs. Richard Kenworthy	1		Mr E Plumb			25
E Cratterton	2		Mr J Ladue			25
Louis Smith	1		*Col. by Mrs. Jos. Faulkner, Wappi's Falls.*			
John Cornell		50	Mr J Faulkner		10	
Henry Hoag	3		Mr Mesiers		10	
George P Dunkin	3		Misses Sweet & Harcourt		10	
Gideon Vincent	1		Occupants Dutchess print shops		30	75
Samuel Moore	1		Mr Nicholas		5	
Jonathan Ham	3		Mr D McKinly		5	
Velie Losee		50	Mr H W Armstrong		3	
Crumaline Dean	2		Mr J Dubois		1	
Arthur Lyon	1		Dr Mangan, New Hamburgh,		5	
Henry C Downing	2		Mrs Freeman		5	
Simon Velie	1		Mrs John Van Wyck		5	
Egbert White	1		Mrs J Brooks			75
George E Velie	1		Mr P A Mesier		5	
John L Brown	2		Mr Walter Millard		5	
Wm Meddangh	1		Mr Wm Millard		2	
Charles Davis	1		Mr Washington Hull		3	
Cash	5		Mr Wm Shay		3	
John Van Benschoten	1		Mr J V Hasbrouck, Hughsonville,		5	
Robert Titus	2		Mr S Dorland		2	
New Hackensack Society.			Mrs H Jones		5	
Mrs C Van Cliff	5		Mrs A Conklin		5	
Mrs O Angel	2		J C Rose		1	
Mrs S Hitchcock	1		Mr James C Dearin		2	
Mrs C Wheaton		25	Mrs H Myers		1	
Mrs J Baker	1		J R V V Dall		1	
Mrs Wm Baker	1		Mr George E Purdy			50
Miss S A Bronson		50	Mr James W P Lamson		1	
Mr Wm Robinson	1		Mrs W Elbricks		5	
Mr J R Vanderbilt	2		Cash		1	
Mr S L Dearin	5		*Fishkill Landing.*			
Mr J Dearin	5		Col Howland		100	
Mr J V B Conklin	2		G W Gitchell		6	

Red Hook (town), col. by Mrs J C Cruger.

Mrs Wm B Astor	$100
Mrs J Swift Livingston	50
Mrs Henry Livingston	50
Mrs Alex Van Rensselaer	50
Mrs John C Cruger	50
Mr Wm L Chamberlin	25
Mr A J Cipnant	20
Mrs C L Barker	10
Mrs Donaldson	10

Red Hook, col. by Mrs John Lewis.

Mrs R L Massonneau	5
Mrs B C Massonneau	5
Mrs A Allendorf	3
Mr J Curtis	2
Mr W S Curtis	2
Mr H Conklin	2
Mrs Benedict	3
Mrs J Bates	3
Mrs S Nelson	5
Miss M Bonesteel	2
Mrs Bonesteel & Atwill	5
Mrs s Elmendorf	3
Mrs E Elmendorf	2
Miss A Pitcher	1
Mrs Abram Pitcher	1
Mrs W Pitcher	1
Mrs W Moore	1
Mrs J R Ecrley	3
Mr Rockfeller	1
Mr J Frdeigh	1
Mrs G Fraleigh	2
Mrs Hendricks	5
Mr P G Fraleigh	5
Mr W S Martin	2
Mrs N P Tyler	1
Miss Jackson	2
Misses Elseller	4
Mrs Collin	2
Mrs Moore	1
Mrs Gase	1
Mrs Hart	1 50
Miss Hevenor	1
Mrs H Barringer	50
Mr B Hevenor	1
Miss Shaffer	50
Mrs Teator	1
Mrs Teats	1
Mrs Pinder	1
Mrs Shultz	2
Mrs Hoffman	1
Mrs Pulver	1
Miss Pulver	1
Cash	3 50
Miss Moore	1
Mrs G Barringer	1

	$	C0
Mrs Crandell		
Mrs G Straat	2	
Mr Wheeler	1	
Mr Waldorph	2	
Mrs J N Lewis	5	
Mrs Wm Lasher	1	

Rhinebeck

Mrs Wm Kelly	35
Mr H Delomater	20
Mrs Caroline Dennison	10
M Nelson	3

Union Vale Cash Donations.

Mr George E Yeomans	5
Mr George C Germond	5
By Miss H Collin—A H Coffin	3
Mrs G W Allerton	2
Dr D Knapp	1
Mr R V Hall	1

Pawling Cash Donations.

Hon J B Dutcher	25
Mrs Harmon Bancroft	43 50
Mr Nathaniel Pearce	5
Mrs George P Tabor	35
Mr Oliver A Tabor	2

Stanford Cash Donations.

Mr Isaac S Carpenter	10
Mrs Cornelius Pugsley	10
Mrs Henry Tallmadge	1
Mr Rufus Smith	60

Wash'ton (town), col by Mrs Milton Ham.

Mr Jeremiah Cooper	2	
Mr Jonas Cooper	2	
Mrs Wm Tabor	2	
Mr Stephen D Smith	2	
Mary Lyon	1	
Mr Daniel Sands	1	
Mr George H Brown	50	
Anna M Haviland	3	
Mr Reuben S Haight	2	
Mr Thomas Howard	1	
S M Hathaway	5	
J Wintringham	5	
B Griffin	2	
Ann K Thorn	5	
Cash	2	
Joshua Simmons	1	
Hiram Sutherland	2	
Cash	1	
Cash	2	
David Mitchell	1	
Milton Ham	5	
Collected by Miss L Collin	13	
" " Miss Cotlin	1	

Dutchess Co. Room One Hundred Years Ago.

The most attractive and most profitable single feature of this Fair was a "Dutchess County Room of one hundred years ago." Crowds thronged it day and evening, and for the moderate sum of ten cents admission fee, and fifty cents for a "tea" in the rural style of a hundred years ago, the receipts were very large.

The exterior of one side of a spacious house was seen. The double door was adorned with a knocker which had done service one hundred and twenty years at a mansion near Poughkeepsie. The ticket-holder would use it, when the upper door would open and a pretty waiting maid would appear, dressed in ancient petticoat and short gown. She received the visitor and his ticket and opened his way into the mansion. What a change! Overhead was a low ceiling with huge projecting beams, on one of which hung a fowling piece and powder horn at least a century old. Before him was a huge fire place, ornamented with old Dutch tiles, on which, in blue color, were illustrations of Scripture history. Over the mantel-shelf were hung silhouette likenesses, a "bull's eye" watch, etc. Upon it were ancient plain flower-vases and other now obsolete ornaments, antique candlesticks, a tobacco-pouch, and a few other things; and below it were two immense Holland tobacco-pipes. On the wainscoting of the jamb was a "Poor Richard's Almanack," 1774. On one side of the fire-place was an ancient "corner cupboard," filled with antique china of all kinds, from the small tea-cup to the spacious punch-bowl. On the other side was an old English clock in tall mahogany case, and a delicate ebony candle-stand. There was also a spinnet, the musical instrument of two centuries ago, out of which grew the harpsichord and the piano forte. There was a sofa brought into Dutchess County from Holland in 1690; and more than a dozen old chairs of as many patterns. Two old mirrors, one of them with candelabra attached, reflected the scenes. The walls were hung with ancient pictures and "samplers," some of them brought from Holland; and upon a high shelf were about a dozen books, most of them printed in Holland and bound in vellum, and none less than a century old. Upon a small antique table lay a fine old Dutch Bible with silver clasps; and upon a peg hung a scarlet cloak and a turkey-down tippet, both made in the middle of the last century. A sword, with pistol attached, used in the French and Indian war, hung on a hook; and in one part of the room was a large round dining-table of solid mahogany, brought from Holland at the beginning of the last century, at which Washington and many distinguished men of the Revolution had sat. The windows were shaded with curtains which did service in the country before the Revolution. The entire wood-work of the apartment was of the somber red-brown peculiar to old dwellings. Scarcely an article in the room was less than one hundred years old. Such was its "still life."

Most attractive of all was the family who inhabited the room during the Fair. It was composed of ladies, some of them members of some of the oldest families on the Hudson. They were all dressed in the costumes of their grandmothers or great-grandmothers—the genuine dresses, full a hundred years old. One was seen merrily spinning on the great wool-wheel; another making thread with an ancient flax-wheel; and another, as the mistress of the house, presided at the tea-table—the ancient one just mentioned—whereon might be seen an abundance of the silver, pewter and china vessels and plates of the olden time, with the substantials and dainties that lay on a thrifty housewife's table in those days, and the lump of sugar suspended by a string, that the tea-drinker might choose to "stir or bite." Moving about with dignity was seen an apparent guest of the family, in the costume of Mrs. Washington when she was Martha Castis, in 1755. Others of the family were engaged in proper duties. A bright and stirring Dutch housekeeper preserved order in domestic affairs. Serenity was personified in the quiet demeanor of a sweet Quakeress in her grandmother's drab silk dress; while the aborigines were represented by an Indian girl in full costume, wearing on her arm an embossed silver band, which was taken from an Indian grave on one of the Thousand Islands of the St. Lawrence. To make the group complete, in the chimney-corner sat gray-haired Pompey in patriarchal dignity, in small-clothes and scarlet waistcoat. Thus every ingredient of society in Dutchess County a hundred years ago was represented.

LIST OF FURNITURE, &c.

Iron Pot which belonged to some of Rochambeau's troops—Mrs. Buckingham.
Quilt 100 years old—Mrs. Fisher. Wine Glass—Mrs. Fisher.
Chintz Curtains—Mrs. Wm. S. Morgan.
Antique Bag and Picture—Mrs. Costar.
Fine high heeled and brocade Shoes—Mrs. R. Mitchell.
Fine Shoes, silk pieced Chair, Teaspoons—Mrs. Utter.
Linen Curtain, China Cup and Saucer 200 year old—Mrs. Utter.
Sword, with pistol attached, used in the old French War—Mrs. Ellsworth.
Antique Box, Andirons, blue satin quilted Petticoat 200 ys old—Mrs. Ellsworth.
Tables, Chairs, China Tea-Set, Punch Bowl Mrs. C. H. Ruggles.
Vases, Tea Tray, Coffee Urn—Mrs. C H. Ruggles.
Old Looking Glass and Clock—Mrs. B. J Lossing.
Old Chair from Washington's Headquarters, Pawling—Mrs. B. J. Lossing.
Fine gilt Looking Glass, candelabra attached—Mrs. James Wilkinson.
Mahogany Table and Sofa, brought from Holland—M. Vassar, jr.
Picture from Holland and Treatise on Trees—Mr. Johnston
Candle Stand—Joseph Flagler.
Dutch Tiles—Mrs. Stephen Thorn.
Turkey down Tippet and Watch—Mr. Lawrence.
Silhouettes, Old Pitcher and samplers—Mark Farrand.
Fine China Bowl and Cup and Saucer—Mrs. E. Van Kleeck.
Skirt, Shortgown, Linen Apron, Cap and Saucer 200 years old—Mrs. Scofield.
China Cups and Saucers, Milk-pot, Tea-pot—Miss M Haviland, Hartsville.
Standard Plate, Pewter Platter and Plates—   "   "   "
Cup and Saucer 200 years old—Spinet 180 years—Mr. G. T. Brown.
China Milk-pot—Miss Tenney.
China Tea-pot 200 years old—Miss C Fonda.
Cup and Saucer—Mrs. H. Swift
Vases, Bowl and Pitcher—Mrs. W. H. Crosby.
Chairs—Miss Harvey.
Scarlet Cloak—Mrs. Weddle.
Watch—Mrs. DeGroff.
Pictures—Mr. J. P. Donw.
Pictures and Pipes—Dr. Beadle.
Large Spinning Wheel—Mrs T. W. Tallmadge.
Small Wheel—Mrs. Brown, La Grange.
Long Gun—M. Z. Dubois, Ulster Co.
Pewter Dish and Plates—Dr. Gill.
Pewter Platters and Plates—Mrs. D. S. Jones.
Silver Tea pot and Milk pot, Brass Knocker—Mrs. H. Livingston.
Pewter Platters and Plates—   "   "
Pewter Dish Mrs. Buck.
Pewter Platters— Mr. Yelverton.
Pewter Platter— T. Gregory.
Powder Horn—B. Southwick.
Corner Cupboard—N. Donaldson.
Ornamented Silver Snuff Box and Bible—Mr. L. M. Arnold.

Fine Bible with clasps, from Holland—Mr. D. B. Lent.
Dr. Franklin's Almanac for 1754, 9 ancient Holland volumes B. J. Lossing.
Medical Work—J. F. Merritt, Pleasant Plains.
Sampler—Mrs. Matthew J. Myers.

The above articles were all within the old Dutchess County Room. The list is incomplete, as a number of articles were not registered by those who loaned them. Many articles were offered which from lack of space could not be accepted. A complete silver tea set that once belonged to Judge Bloom, of this county, was among the most valuable. Besides articles of furniture, the ladies have to thank many for articles of ancient dress. A curiously quilted petticoat was lent by Mrs. Sarah Ferris, of Quaker Hill. The Indian costume came, in part, from the western Indian reserve in this State; two complete antique suits were loaned by Mrs. Judge Vanderbilt, Flatbush, L. I., and two others were sent from Albany. High heeled and elegant shoes, buckles, shortgowns, lawn aprons, quilted petticoats and other antique clothes, more than could be used, were loaned for the purpose of being worn in the old room, and the ladies have to render thanks to their owners for the alacrity with which these time-honored relics and heir-looms were tendered for the benefit of the Sanitary Fair. Nearly all of the articles used in the old room were fully a century old, while some reached the age of 200 years.

Mrs. D. S. Jones was one of the ladies who presided in the "Dutchess County Room of 100 years ago." She was dressed in ancient costume, received the guests, and did the honors at the Dutch Tea Table. She was assisted by Mrs. C. H. Ruggles, in a Dutch dress, who also presided at the large wool wheel.

Miss Henrietta Livingston, in a rich brocade dress and high heeled shoes of her great-grandmother, added much to the attractions of the room. Mrs. Levi M. Arnold, dressed as Martha Custis, presided with dignity, and was much admired, while Mrs. E. Beck delighted the visitors by her spinning on the flax wheel. Miss Carrie Patten was quite attractive in her pretty Dutch dress, and Mrs. Franklin as a Dutch housekeeper performed her part extremely well. Mrs. Lossing as Eunice Manwee the last of the Pequods, in full Indian costume, was perfect. Mr. and Mrs. Lossing also appeared in the full dress of the last century, and were greatly admired. Miss Broom wore a dress 200 years old, with high heeled satin shoes and large paste buckles of her great-great-grandmother, with old lace and jewels to correspond. Mrs. Ruggles contributed to the corner cupboard some rare old family antiquities once used by her Dutch ancestors, among them a china vase brought to this country in the year 1670. Miss Varick appeared in a dress belonging to her family, 100 years old; and Miss Degrott as porteress in a dress 95 years old. The Dutchess County Room was built and arranged by Mr. and Mrs. B. J. Lossing, and was perfect in all respects. Mr. Matthew Vassar, jr., devoted himself to it, and aided the ladies greatly in its success.

THE "SKATING POND"

was located at the west end of the third story, opposite the *Dutch*-ess County Room of 100 years ago. To this and a collection of relics and curiosities was assigned a space some fifteen by twenty feet. The windows and walls, here, were decorated with American Flags and Bunting, arranged with some taste and in more profusion, while excellent paintings, banners, uniforms, swords and fire arms, possessing historical value from their connection with the Revolution or the Rebellion were also scattered around freely.

On entering, the visitor found upon his right a large glass case completely filled with rare and interesting curiosities and relics, the contribution of Benson J. Lossing, Esq. Over this was a map of the United States in silk needlework, so perfectly executed that it was generally mistaken for an engraving. This was executed in 1800 by Mrs. Cary, still a resident of Poughkeepsie.

Next to the case was the model of a cottage, its interior provided with miniature furniture, and its door yard with a miniature fountain of *real* water, supplied by a reservoir concealed in a moss-covered castle adjoining the house. This was the work and contribution of Mr. Hobart Schroeder, of Hyde Park.

Near this was the Skating Pond, constructed under the supervision of Mrs. E. Anthony, of Brooklyn, the lady whose devotion to the cause of the soldier induced her to provide the same exhibition for the Brooklyn and New York Fairs. A familiar illustration will be a sufficient description of its construction and operation. Let us suppose the sides—inside—of a common washing tub to be lined with plates of looking glass, each about six inches wide and extending from the rim to the bottom of the tub; then put in a false bottom, arranged to revolve upon a central pin which raises it a little above the real bottom; cover this false bottom with ice-colored glass, put upon it some doll figures, in skating costumes, and set it in motion. By placing the eyes near the rim of the tub and looking at the reflections in the mirrors on the opposite side, the visitor sees a very perfect picture of a large Skating Pond with skaters in full motion.

Not far removed from this was a table whereat silver coin was freely exchanged for government currency of equal amount, provided the applicant would hold a certain brass ball in one hand while he removed the coveted coin from a basin of water with the other.

Next was found a large assortment of mementoes of the Rebellion, relics and mineralogical specimens " too numerous to mention," the surface of a very large table being entirely covered with them.

The last, though not least, of the attractions of this attractive room was a glass case filling the space of a cubic yard. It contained a wind-mill, steam engine and water wheel, which, though made of sugar, were in constant motion. The sign board on the wind-mill building proclaimed it to be a

"PATENT MILL FOR MAKING OLD LADIES YOUNG."

On one side was seen a number of old ladies who, having entered the premises through the gate, were offering their money in payment for the proposed transformation—one holding up for the purpose a purse of $1,000. Two flight of stairs led, on the outside, to the top of the mill, and therein, head-foremost, had been plunged one aged dame, the miller still standing over her, pushing down a refractory limb which still projected, and, to little purpose, beat the air. At another point was seen an "intelligent contraband" shaping a pretty face with a drawing knife, and at another a mechanic busied with some other portion of the previous subject. Finally is seen a yard full of bewitching demoiselles, who have been entirely through the transforming process, and seem pleased enough with their bargains as they welcome the exit of the last-changed-one from the open door of the mill.

This curious work of science and art was contributed by Mr. Anderson, the confectioner in Brooklyn, who had previously exhibited it at the Brooklyn Fair, where it was very much admired.

Our glance through this portion of the Fair has been brief, but it is a source of much pleasure to be able to say that visitors generally expressed themselves well repaid for both money and time by glances at the reality no less hasty than this one with pen and ink. A whole day might have been profitably occupied in examining the contents of the "Skating Pond Room."

THE FLORAL TEMPLE

occupied the centre of the south side of the hall. It was arranged by Mrs. Davies, in a tasteful style, and was an object of especial attraction during the Fair. It was supported by columns wreathed with evergreens and flowers, and draped with the stars and stripes. On the interior of either side were plate glass mirrors and tables, on which were exhibited every description of bouquets; flowers in baskets, flowers in vases, flowers in pots, and all the lovely family of flowers.

Ladies' Receiving Committee Report.

FANCY DEPARTMENT.

Van Valkenburgh & Brown, 3 dozen bottles of Perfume, 6 bottles of Tricopherous, 2 Toilet Bottles, 2 Pomatum Bottles, 39 Cakes of Soap.
Miss Webster, Feather Work.
Miss Kitty Northrop, 1 pair of Drawers, 1 mat.
Mrs. Henry Sterling, Beckman, 5 baskets of Flowers, 1 Emery Cushion.
Mrs. Wm. C. Barnes, Sofa Pillow.
Miss Sheldon, vase of Wax Flowers.
Mrs. Costar, Sofa Pillow, Likeness of Prince of Wales, Bracelet.
Mrs. Rose, Geneva, Pin Cush., Brioche.
Miss Macomb, 2 Pin-Cush's, 1 mouchoir.
Miss H J Pollock, piece of Lace, 2 Parlor Balls.
Miss Sheldon, 2 Bead mats.
Mrs. T. C. Campbell, Davenport, Iowa, Opera Hood.
Miss Mary Broom, Dolls, Afghan.
Mary E. Collins, Pen Wiper, Sleeves, 3 Needle Books.
Mrs. Reuben North, Tidy, Lace Collar.
No Name, 2 H'dkerchief Cases, 2 Glove Cases, 4 large, 12 small Cushions, 2 Bean Bags, 3 pairs Slippers, 4 mats, 1 Needle Book, 2 dolls.
Miss A. Jones, Stanford, 2 Collars.
Miss S. Trowbridge, Cushion.
Miss A. Hopkins, Cushion.
Mrs. J. Sands, 5 Bows, 4 Quakers, 4 Pen Wipers, 1 pair of Slippers.
Mrs. Platt Ketcham, box of Jewelry.
Mrs. L Canfield, Pleas't Valley, Lemon, box Jewelry.
Miss A Hendrickson, Bag, 2 mats.
Miss M Foster, Cush'n, Collar, Emery.
Miss A. Schoonover, 2 Collars
Miss Elma Sands, Needle Book.
Miss E. Foster, 3 Cushions, Watch Case, Needle Book.
Miss S. Ketcham, Collar and Tie, 2 Cane Baskets, Cone Mat, Cus'n, Pen Wiper.
Mrs. E. Parker, Collar and Cuffs.
Mrs. Arnold, 2 Tents.

Mrs. A. Merritt, Washington, Slippers, Infant's Socks, Child's Sash, Box.
Mrs. Porter, Slippers.
Miss Evans, Titusville, Traveling Bag.
Miss Cora Dean, LaGrange, Pin Cush'n.
Jennie Hasbrouck, Cushion, 2 pairs Infant's Socks, Lines, Book-mark
Ida Banker, Doll.
Mrs. Bailey, 2 Linen Bonnets, 2 Aprons.
Mrs. G. S Wells, Pin Cushion.
John W. Barratt & Co., Fancy Art. $12.
No Name, Vase, 3 Work Boxes, Cush'n, Parlor Ball.
Miss Kate Mott, Book-mark, Ham Basket.
Mrs. Eastman, pair Slippers.
Mrs. Eastman and Harvey, Afghan.
Miss Pickford, Cone Basket, Apron.
Miss Kate Pickford, Rice Basket, Inf't's Socks.
Mrs. Rapp, Port Folio.
Mrs. Mary Freeman, Feather Flowers.
Mrs. Dr. Thompson, 4 Elephants.
Miss Susan Swift, (a deaf mute,) 3 vases Wax Flowers.
Miss A. E. Frost, Sofa Cus', 2 prs Socks.
Amenia, Cone Basket, 2 Cus'ns, Child's Waist, 3 pairs Stockings, 1 Bed Quil , 6 Neck Ties, 2 Handkerchief Cases, 3 Watch Cases, 1 pair Infant's Socks, 3 Aprons, 1 Transparency, Parlor Ball.
Susan Knapp, Beckman, Table Cloth.
Mrs. F. Davis, 6 Pin Cushions, Melon Hood, Card Basket.
Mrs. B. C. Meeks, mat, 4 prs Porcupine Vases.
No Name, 1 moss Box, 1 Cone Box.
Rhinebeck Reformed Dutch Cause , Traveling Cases, 1 Parlor Ball, Brook fast Cap, 5 pairs Stockings, Crib Spd, Shawl, Rigolette, 6 Tidies, Pen Wiper, Knit Shirt, Apr'n, 2 Book-marks, Bag, Fan, 7 Cus'ns, 2 Collars, Worked Set, 2 mats, Emery, Shawl Pin, 2 Needle Books, Box, Porte monnaie.
Helen Robinson, Fishkill Plains, Cus'n.

Adelia Robinson, Tidy.
Lottie Robinson, 2 pairs Infant's Socks.
Mary Trowbridge, Set of mats.
Alice Coggswell, 3 Pin Cushions.
Mary Brown, Pin Cushions.
Miss Cordelia Allen, 2 Baskets.
Mrs J E Allen, Baby's Socks.
Mrs Willard H Crosby, Cushion.
Miss Josie Brown, Pleas't Valley, Tidy.
Miss Mary and Anna Allen, Slippers and 2 Baskets.
Benson J Lossing, 50 copies of the Van Kleeck House.
No Name, 11 Cushions, 2 Book-marks, 2 Pen Wipers, Collar.
Miss Emma Sleight, Bead Collar, 3 Book marks.
Lona Eschinger, Infant's Dress—material furnished by Friends.
Mrs Degroff, Wax Doll, Boy Doll, 2 Infant's Waists, Doll's Dress, 2 Yokes and Sleeves.
T T Spencer, 4 Autograph Books.
Miss F Jones, Sofa Pillow.
Mary A McLean, Bead Mat.
W Berry, Wax Doll, dressed by Mrs E Cary.
Miss Coffin, Washington, 2 pairs mats, Tetting, Needle Book, Slippers.
Miss Jessie Nelson. 2 Mats.
Miss Kate Van Keuren, 2 Watch Cases, Slippers.
Miss Mary Smart, Chair, 2 Picture Frames, 7 Engravings, manuscript.
Mrs F S Phinney, 2 Knit Shawls.
Mrs Parker, 2 Hoods, 6 Infant's Shirts.
Mrs J P Adriance, 2 Lines, Waist and Drawers.
Rev J L Corning, Sword Cane captured by Gen Butler at N. O.
Mrs Clegg, Cushion.
Anna Dodge, 2 Paper Holders.
R P Morgan jr., Toilet Set.
Mrs E Van Valkenburgh, House-Wife, Pen Wiper, 2 Inf's Drawers, 2 Doll's Toilet Tables, 2 Doll's Brioche, Leath. Work Set.
Miss Rita Van Valkenburgh, 3 Quaker Dolls, Doll's Brioche.
Miss Anna Frost, Inf't's Blanket, Socks.
Miss Purdy, Spool Wagon, G P Wipers, 11 Pin Cush's, Knitting Needle Case.
S M Welker, 2 meerschaums.
Miss E F Barnes, Miss Maria Barnes and Miss E Barnes, Toilet Set, 2 Infant's Shirts, 3 Infant's Socks.
Miss Storm, Toilet and Dinner mats.
Miss Maggie Wilson, Breakfast Shawl, Scarf.
Mrs A A Underhill, Watch Case, Twilight.
The Misses Livingston, 2 Pen Wipers, 2 Pin Cushions, 4 Dolls. Chair, 2 pairs Infant's Shoes, 2 Knitting Aprons, 2 Slippers, Sack, 5 mats, Smok'g Cap, Sack.
Mrs George Carson, 2 mats.
Miss Mary Carson, 2 mats.
Fisher Carson, Collar.

Mrs F W G Jones, Tidy.
Geo H Beatty's, 7 Gent's Scarf, 2 dozen Neck Ties, 100 Boxes Collars.
Mrs A J Currier, Slippers, Embroidered Flannel Skirt.
R Taylor, 3 doz. boxes magnetic Oint't.
Mrs James G Wood, Tidy, 2 pairs Lines.
Nellie M Swift, Washington, 2 Flags, Tidy, 6 yards Edging.
Mrs B Mitchell, 6 Rabbits.
Miss Warring, Breakfast Shawl, Tidy, 7 Pen Wipers, 3 Infant's Socks, 2 Bibs.
Miss Broom, 2 pairs Slippers.
Amanda Germond, 6 Wash Cloths, Slippers, Shur Bag.
Addie Overton, Looking Glass, Chinese Box, 2 Book-marks, Glass Basket.
Sarah Overton, Chinese Box, Glass Basket, Book-mark, Flower Pot, Basket.
Sarah Bishop, 2 Table d'oyleys, Crochet Collar, Needle Book.
H H Bishop, 4 yards Tetting Insertion, 4 yards Edge.
Mrs Wm Rowe, 2 Tidies, Slipp's, Watch Case, Bed Quilt.
Mrs J Ellsworth, Toilet Set, Pin Cus'n, 6 pairs Infant's Shoes, Embr'd Pillow Covers, 3 d'oyley, 2 Cups, 3 Shaving Papers.
Minnie Pettit, Infant's Shoes.
Mrs Ayrault, House-Wife, Pin Cushion, 2 Shoe Bags, 5 Scissor Cases, Spectacle Case.
Mr Cornwell, 6 papers of Pins and roll of Wrapping Paper.
L M Ferris and family, 3 Lamp Shades, pair Slippers, Sacks, 6 Pen Wipers, 8 Dolls, 3 Book-marks, Pin Cushion, 2 Parlor Balls, 2 Needle Books, Case of Fancy Photographs.
Mrs James Taylor, Locust Glen, 4 pairs of Worsted Cuffs.
Miss Annie Brown, Worsted Tidy.
Miss M Arnold, Pin Cus'n, Sofa Cus'n.
Miss N Pierce, Tidy.
Miss E Chapman, Tidy, Collar, pr mats.
Miss S Doty, 3 Thimble Cases, Spool Case.
Mrs F Chapman, Yoke & Sleeves, Needle Book, 2 Pin Balls.
Miss Susy Stark, Pin Cushion, Doll.
L M Pierce, Toilet Set.
Miss T A Stark, Table mats, Smo'g Caps.
Mrs W Taber, Apron.
Mrs B Pierce, Tidy, Fortune Teller.
Mrs J W Stark, Pin Cushion.
Miss S Kirby, Tidy, Yoke and Sleeves, Handkerchief, Pin Cushion, 4 Needle Books, 2 mats, 2 Pen Wipers.
Sarah Wing, Child's Cap, pair mats, Tidy, 2 Pen Wipers, Ruler.
Mrs E Wanzer, Cushion.
Mrs G Kirby, Tidy, Wristlets.
Miss S Doughty, 3 Thimble Cases, 2 Spool Cases.
Miss Fannie Kirby, Tidy, 5 Pin Cus'us.
Miss Sarah Akin, mat.
Miss Anna Akin, Sofa Pillow, 2 Spool Cases, 3 Emery Cush'ns, 6 Pin Balls.

Miss Libby Vanderburgh, 3 Needleb'ks.
Mrs J A Baily, 2 Shirts.
Miss Emma Bailey, pair mats.
Miss Eliza Ferris, 2 dolls, 2 needleb'ks.
Mrs Betsy Toffey, Quaker Hill, p cus'n.
Mrs James Craft, sofa pillow.
The Misses Craft, set of jewelry.
Mrs John Toffry, pair of mittens.
Miss R A Chase, pair of slippers.
Mrs N Kerr, oriental painting.
Mrs Helen R Taber, 2 pin cushions, 2 mats, infant's bib, handkerchief holder, 2 pairs slippers, 2 razor cases.
Miss F Kirby, 3 book-marks, 2 mats, 5 razor cases, slippers.
Mrs J A Taber, 2 work baskets, 6 work cases.
Miss Annie Tweedy, cape, tidy, pair slippers, doll.
Miss Amy Kirby, 2 dolls.
Mrs Edward Wanzer, doll, watch case, riggolette.
Mrs George P Taber, 2 dolls.
Mrs George K Taber, Afghan.
Miss H Taber, apron.
Miss S Sherman, Washington, child's waist.
Miss C Sherman, child's bibs, 4 rabbits.
Charlie Adams, 6 Brackets.
Mrs Faulkner, pair slippers, 2 needle cases, 2 sofa cushions, brioche.
Miss Emily Arnold, pair mats.
The Independent Club, composed of the following ladies: Mrs Jas Reynolds, Mrs Edwin Marshall, Mrs Daniel Thompson, Mrs L M Vincent, Mrs Dr Harvey, Mrs W Johnson, Mrs Dr Hasbrouck, Mrs J A Jillson, Mrs G T Brown, Mrs Hedding, Mrs J H Coggswell, Mrs Henry Morgan, Mrs Chas Storm, Mrs L Johnson—8 children's ap'ns, 4 ladies' ap'ns, pair undersleeves, 6 shirt waists, 9 night caps, chair tidy, sofa tidy, basket bag, 3 what nots, 7 y'ds edging, 4½ yards tape trimming, 2 crosses framed, hood, toilet set, pin cush'n, 4 paintings.
Indefatigable Club, composed of the following ladies: Miss Martha Reynolds, Miss Mary Reynolds, Miss Jennie Collingwood, Miss Frank Clark, Miss Eugenie Collingwood, Miss Julia Clark, Miss Hannah M Southwick, Miss Mary Vincent, Miss Sarah Harris, Miss Grace Reynolds, Miss Allie Lent, Miss Mary L Reynolds—13 pin cushions, Turkey pin cushion, 14 dolls, 2 breakfast capes, 4 Infant's bibs, chair, 4 tidies, needleb'k, fancy work, bag, 8 infant's sacks, 97 pairs slippers, 16 mats, 2 baby's bands, 5 pairs of lines, 5 needle books, setting yoke and sleeves, 5 pairs of mittens, 3 toilet sets, 15 pocket pin cushions, sofa cushion, 2 pairs invalid shoes, hood, 14 pen wipers, 3 watch cases, 2 night dress holders, baby socks, rabbit, 6 parlor balls, 2 old ladies.
Miss Dubois and Miss Flint, lot of fancy articles, crochet collar, pen wiper, &c.
Miss A Smith, 4 bookmarks, p cushion.

Robert Schreder, fancy cottage and fountain.
Mrs Heydock, 2 summer hoods, 6 Infant's shirts.
Mrs Josie Brown, Pleasant Valley, netted tidy.
Susie E Fenwick, 6 jumping dolls.
Miss Wright and Southwick, 4 pin cushions, 11 pen wipers, book-mark, 3 boy dolls, 2 what nots, 1 doll cushion.
Mrs James and Miss Phinney, child's afghan.
Mrs Colonel Bailey, needle book.
Miss Coffin, hood, 2 rose mats.
Miss Kate Wilkinson, parlor ball.
Mr Freer, boy's cap, miniature hat.
Mrs Walter Corlies, yoke and sleeves, cushion, apron, toilet set, pair mats, pair lines, 6 spectacle wipers.
Clinton, dressing case, shaving case.
Washington, cushion, 5 pairs stockings, toilet case.
Mrs A Baker, Beekman, pair stockings.
Miss M W Adriance, sofa pillow, 3 breakfast shawls, pen wiper, 12 cus'ns.
Miss Addie Fowler, 4 pen wipers, 2 book-marks.
Mr Wilson, 2 transparencies, books $32 95.
Miss Mary Johnson, baby's sack, 2 ties, pen wipers.
Mrs S J Farnum, 6 parlor balls.
Mrs B N Morgan, toilet set.
Mr Franklin, hanging basket.
Mrs Clinton Jones, 3 dolls, 6 cushions, basket, bk-mark, sofa pillow, 3 spool wagons, 3 p'rs Infant's socks, crochet collar, 3 walnut bags, 2 mats, 2 pen wipers.
Ella and Kittie Arnold, 2 pen wipers, 17 Lubin's extracts, raisin turtles.
Miss Charlotte Davies, slippers, camp stool.
Miss Fisher Carson, slippers.
2 pen wipers, cushion.
Mr Philip Winter, 24 pocket books.
Mr J Bajer, 100 cigars.
S H Maxon, cigars.
Mr Rescher, shawl.
Miss Hatch, swifts made by a captain of whaler, during a voyage, of the bones and teeth of a whale.
Mrs T L Davies, vase shell flowers, sofa pillow.
Mrs E V R Cruger, Union slippers.
Mrs Franklin Delano, cushion, pair of slippers, thermometer, papepsic, 2 card cases.
Mrs Barwood, mouchoir case, 2 work bags, 2 butter flies.
Mrs Allen, 3 baby sacks.
Mrs Ingersoll, camp chair.
Miss Ingersoll, 4 pairs line, pen wiper, 4 shoe bags.
A Friend, 2 mats, 3 caps, tidy, watch case.
Mrs Dr Taylor, shell bag, tidy.
Miss C Hulme, 3 handkerchiefs.
Mrs Hulme, child's dress.

Mr R V Cable, 3 gent's slippers, 8 pen wipers, bridal corset.

Miss Jennie N Mills, slippers.

Miss Stephenia Barnes, Pl't Valley, tidy.

Mrs Hutchings, 3 fly cages.

Miss V Rowe, 3 breakfast shawls.

Mrs Orin Williams, embr'd suspenders.

Miss H Wickes, sontag breakfast shawl, child's sack.

Miss C Wickes, gent's scarf, child's bib, child's blanket, skin of eider duck, pen stand.

Mrs C H S Williams, 2 scrap bags, child sash, breakfast shawl, pen wiper, 2 pin cushions.

Mrs J C Holley, book-mark, 4 charter frames.

..ladies'at Mrs Myers, 12 inf's shoes, ...kets Florida grass, 4 slippers, 2 infant's sacks, collar, work box, sack, spectacle case, 3 pin cushions, 2 pen wipers, candy box, basket, mat.

Mrs Dubois, work box, pin cushion, 6 spool racks.

A Friend, sleeves, 3 infant sacks.

Cora Lossing, 2 infant's sacks, bib.

Josie Whaler, scarf, lines, bracket, mats.

Mrs Geo W Sterling, 2 pairs mittens, 2 pairs lines, 2 dozen rabbits.

Mrs Sherman, large cushion.

A W Palmer, Amenia, shawl.

Miss C Van Wyck, mat.

Miss Fannie Swift, Carrie Swift and Charlie Swift, mat, pair baby socks, pair baby socks.

Mrs Dr White, 2 toilet sets.

Miss H R Kipp, 2 pairs slippers.

Miss O White, 2 spool wagons.

Miss Anna Stripple, yoke and sleeves.

Miss R W Stripple, embroidered strip of muslin.

Mrs M J Marshall, Salt Point, 2 work bags, 2 needle books, pin cushion.

Miss P H Marshall, tidy.

Miss Annie Whaler, sacque, tidy, lines.

Miss Sweet, sofa cushion.

Mrs Putnam, 4 pictures.

Mrs John D Wilber, Clinton, 3 needle books, 2 pin cushions.

Mrs Mark D Wilber, shawl.

E Beach, 6 gross buttons.

Mrs A C Boardman, 2 pairs mats, 4 baskets, needle case, 2 pairs slippers, 2 pairs comb cases, 2 work bags, 2 pen wipers, 8 photograph frames—4 with pictures contrabands, 4 fans, 2 tea caddies, 5 paper boxes, lot of shells, worsted shawl, small turtles, worsted tidy, book-mark.

Mrs C W Darling, 3 stuffed birds, inf't's shoes, 2 watch cases, doll, box wood needle case, picture, pr wristlets, fan, doll's brioche, 2 boxes, card case.

Miss Mary Smith, Pleasant Valley, pair stockings.

Miss Robertson, collar and neck tie, evergreens.

Miss Van Wagner, bead collar, 10 pin cushions, 2 collars, 4 bibs.

Miss Masten, 2 cushions, 9 pocket cushions.

Mrs Tompkins, pair socks.

A Friend, 2 cushions, bag and basket, 7 china ducks.

Miss Tobey, 2 tea-pot holders.

Miss Matilda Degroff, 12 pen wipers, 2 cushions, bead collar.

R C Southwick, 4 morocco skins.

Wm Harloe, 6 black walnut brackets, 12 holiday games.

The Misses Atkins, box of candy toys.

Wm Coldstream, 2 cabinets of minerals.

Miss Mary Emigh, sofa pillow, shell basket, pen wiper.

Mrs Dr Benedict, Red Hook, pair slippers, smoking cap, cushion.

A Friend, 5 children's aprons.

Mrs Caleb Hewlett, Hyde Park, 2 pairs slippers.

Miss Mary Bailey, 6 collars.

No Name, 3 infant's socks.

Miss F B Seaman, 2 bead collars.

Mrs J H Seaman, 3 mats.

No Name, 5 bill cases, pair mats, pair socks.

Mr Reckford, pair lady's shoes.

Nicholas Winter, box segars.

No Name, 3 hoods, 2 pairs knit hose, 2 pairs slippers.

Miss Anna Coffin, pair slippers.

Miss Vanderpool, 6 pen wipers.

Miss Susie E Penwick, 6 jumping dolls.

Miss Tiel, toilet set, 2 inft's socks, mat.

Miss F Tanner, cushion.

Mrs Baker, cush'n, 2 fancy chairs, child shirt, cone basket.

Miss Cora Vassar, fancy chairs, cone basket.

Mrs L T Robertson, Pleasant Valley, cone basket, cone vase, 26 pin cus'ns.

Mrs B F Wiley, bible cushion and tidy.

Mrs A M Robertson, 2 cushions, cone basket, cone watch case.

Miss M S Robertson, 2 pin cushions.

Miss Susie Hyzer, slippers.

Freddy Robertson, boquet.

Carrie Masten, cushion, 2 collars, egg-nest.

Mrs Dr Hasbrouck, infant's robe.

Leonora Osborn, aged 80 years, stock's knit for that sick drummer boy.

Miss Babcock, sofa cushion, pin cush'n, tidy.

Miss Mary Van Benschoten, hood.

Mrs Cornwell, A pair cotton socks knit by a lady 74 years old.

Mrs Edward Crosby, basket, 11 book marks, 2 collars, 2 mats, 2 breakfast shawls.

Miss Ellen Sterling, tidy.

Miss Purdy, pen wiper.

No Name, 4 rabbits, 2 book marks.

Emily and Kate Morris, fancy articles.

Mary Swarthout, 3 book marks.

Mrs Hoag, lamp-shade.

Mrs Fanning, bead basket.

Mrs B F Merritt, Plea't Plains, slippers.

Mrs Williams, mats.

Miss Mary Bogardus, 3 infant's socks.
Miss Mary Adams, 3 sacks.
Mr Leffingwell, miniature marble house
Mrs Stephen B Rogers, Beckman, 2 prs hose.
Miss Maria Van Elton, Pleasant Plains, 2 cone framed pictures.
Miss Grace Abel, 3 fortune tellers.
Miss Sherman, 2 mats, 2 aprons.
Miss Jennie Marshall, slippers.
John I Platt, 8 sets alphabetical puzzles
Mrs G H Muller, lace waist, 3 handkerchiefs, fan, 2 barbes, pearl coiffeur.
Jas E Biddle, 40 cards of distinguished men.
Mrs Col Bailey, for the tree, 2 children's aprons, sun bonnet, 9 perfume bags, emery cushion.
Miss C R Patton, 6 dolls.
Miss Ella Patten, 5 dolls, 3 book-marks, mat.
Miss E Van Kleeck, 2 needle books, pr slippers, 6 pen wipers, 8 book-marks.
Mrs Wm Johnson, what not.
Contributed by society, 13 dolls, 43 cornucopia.
Miss Dibble, 2 yoke and sleeves.
Miss M L Crooke, cushion.
Miss J Crooke, 6 needle books.
Mrs Bogardus, 2 sacks, mat, pr socks, 2 knit shirts.
The Misses Van Kleeck, Mrs Eastman, Mrs A Innis, large afghan.
Miss Mary Case, traveling case, cloud, melon hood, 2 mats.
Miss M Everett, 2 ladies' housewives.
Mrs George Cornwell, 4 sacks, 2 wrappers, pair socks.
Miss Jennie Van Kleeck, 2 hoods.
Mary Varick and Jennie Van Kleeck, child's afghan.
Mrs Sarah Hoag, pin cush'n, needle b'k.
Mrs Wyman, pin cushion.
Miss DeGarmo, yoke and sleeves.
Mrs James Seaman, slippers.
Miss Wyman, 2 collars, 8 chairs, sack.
Libby Colby, 2 mats.
Mrs Colby, 4 aprons, bib, cap.
Mrs W S Wright and daughter, slipp's, mat, Turkish smoking cap.
Lucretia Mott, 3 Quakers, 15 cushions, 2 baskets.
Miss Maria High, cushion.
Mrs Tousey, 9 pocket pin cushions.
Miss Hatch, cone ornament.
Miss Palmer, cone basket.
Mrs Dr Palmer, shell basket.
Miss Mary Varick, tidy, 2 hoods, pin cushion.
Miss Babcock, night cap, 3 prs infant's socks, 2 prs suspend's, 4 needle cases, pin cushion.
Miss Tenney, 3 mats.
Miss Jennie E Thompson, 3 pen wipers, 3 watch cases, 3 pin cushions.
Miss Cora Van Kleeck, tidy, pair mats, hood, 3 fortune tellers.
Miss M Hasbrouck, 2 pairs mats, book mark.

E F Blake, chair.
Miss Susan Sievers, bouquet candy flowers.
Mrs James Hill, toilet cushion, 2 table cushions.
Brooklyn Friend, mouchoir, philopatrian, bandy boy doll, cushion, 3 infant shirts, 2 pairs socks, pr mittens, side combs, engraving, 50 photographs, pr mats, infant's apron, puzzle.
Miss C Fonda, 2 watch cases.
Miss F Fonda, cushion.
Miss Knapp, afghan.
No Name, 3 needle books, pr stockings.
A Friend, chemise, tidy.
Miss C Griffin, tidy, cushion.
Mrs A Wright, sofa cushion, pair mats, 1 dozen cushions, 3 cologne bottles.
Mrs Joseph Wright, book-mark, what not cushion.
Mrs Hawley, Texas, Rose bedquilt.
The Misses Varick, farm house, quilting party, 2 pin cushions, pr mats, toilet set, work box, worsted chair cover, 5 needle books, 4 pen wipers, 4 watch cases, 3 shaving paper holders, pocket handkerchief, 4 pocket cushions.
Miss Alida Varick, pin cushion, 2 crochet bags.
Mrs Oscar A Fowler, Spanish hood, breakfast shawl.
M L Crooke, sofa pillow, 2 p cushions, 6 needle books.
The Misses Beadle, 12 toilet cush'ns, 12 aprons, 12 shoe bags.
Miss Fanning, 4 pin cushions, 30 emery cushions, slippers, 2 pin cushion covers, 2 d'oyley, 9 mats, tidy toilet mats.
Miss Nettie Farnum, 2 pen wipers, knit shirt, sack.
The Misses Parker, 2 pin cushions, 3 p wipers, 2 tidies, balls, 3 shawls, 7 mats, bag, 5 yards tetting, 10 pocket cus'ns.
Misses Johnson and Farnum, child's afghan.
Mrs John P Parker, 50 emery cushions.
Mrs Joseph Ward, Pleasant Valley, 2 pairs socks, book-mark, 2 inf's hoods.
Miss V Ward, Pleasant Valley, tidy.
Miss F Clearwater, Pleasant Valley, wk basket.
Miss J Ward, 2 mats.
Miss Charlotte Cash, Pleasant Valley, 2 Quakers, 11 pocket pin cushions.
Miss Van Benschoten, Pleasant Valley, 2 book-marks.
Henderson & Bro., clock.
Miss Ward, Pleas't Valley, cone basket.
Miss Holden, Pl.Val., infant's bib, tidy.
Mrs E E Sterling, Pl.Val., infant's sack, 3 inf't's ap's, doll bag, tea pot holder.
Miss Mary E Parker, knit shawl, inf't's sack.
Mrs Loraine, Mme Demorest's sewing machine, 6 night dress holders, 2 comb bags, 2 infant's bibs.
Mrs Dr Bolton, neck tie, tidy.
G K Lawrence, vest, neck tie.
Mrs Aaron Innis, afghan.

Mrs Geo Innis, 3 prs slippers, cushion, toilet set, pair lines, 2 needle books.

Mrs Lossing, sofa cushion.

Mrs Charles Wheaton, knit shawl, slippers.

Clara E Schrœder, S E Schrœder and Charles Schrœder, infant's bib, 2 pin cushions, bone basket, wooden book, pocket pin cushion.

Mrs F H Simpson, tidy, 2 pairs mats, pr lines, pin cushion.

No Name, 4 pin cush'ns, slippers, 6 pen wipers, watch case, mat.

Judge Emott, inlaid work box.

Mrs James Emott, Japanese boat, brioche, illuminated prayer.

Miss Laura Emott, 2 baby's bibs.

Mrs Walter Morgan, 2 prs mats, inf's bib.

Miss North, yoke and sleeves.

Miss J Frost and Miss E Frost, 3 mats, tidy, slippers, 5 morocco cases.

Miss Duncan, large mat.

Student's Retreat, 6 pin cushions, 8 flag cushions, work bag, 2 shaving papers, 2 bead collars, 3 mats, 2 apr's, 2 caps, 13 crosses, book mark, boot, wk box, doll, paper basket, wheel barrow, basket flowers, fortune teller.

Sarah Heynton, cone box, watch case.

Miss Carrie Sherman, Cottage Hill, bead pin cushion, pair lines.

Miss Mattie Wickes, bead mat, pr toilet slippers, 2 mats, doll's shawl, Roman scarf.

Miss Sarah Parish, sofa cushion, tidy, pair perfume sackets.

Miss Josephine Doughty, 2 pen wipers, China doll in white opera cloak, red riding hood.

Miss Florence Clark, tidy, crying doll.

Miss Lizzie Wright, Hannah Thurston, cushion, small Quaker, cone basket.

Miss Mary Goodman, 2 pairs mats.

Miss Maria Booth, mouchoir case, music portfolio.

Miss Frances Snyder, velvet slippers, book-mark.

Miss Juliet Smith, work basket, tomato cushion.

Miss Hannah Keese, kid housewife, 3 needle cases, pair infant socks.

Miss Mary Bockee, slipp's, 2 bk-marks.

Miss Lillie Van Nostrand, smoking cap.

Miss Maggie Marcellus, melon hood.

Miss Louisa Hart, pr Scotch plaid slippers.

Miss Bessie Francis, striped shawl.

Miss Ella Warner, white silk braided cushion.

Miss Mary Mulligan, breakfast shawl.

Miss Fannie Vail, pair mats.

Miss Augusta Nichols, baby's c. p.

Miss Clara Slee, tidy.

Miss Helen McIntosh, national tidy.

Miss Sarah Sagendorf, tidy.

Miss Virginia Mulligan, pair rose mats.

Miss Fannie Drew, book-marks.

Miss E S Watson, 2 worsted aprons.

Miss Mary Nichols, Roman scarf.

Miss Susan Myers, d'oyley.

Miss Nellie Barculo, doll in illusion dr's

Miss Mary Van Vleit, 4 small china dolls, book-mark.

Miss Eleanor Moore, 4 parlor balls.

Miss Allie Davies, pair embr'd slippers.

M ss Bell Cornwell, pair braided cloth slippers.

Miss Emily Hart, pr embroi'd slippers.

Miss Bella Sloan, Maggie Reed, Emma Hart, Iva Robbins, Miss Kate Dunberry, Dollie Wandel, G Paigs, Mrs G T Lider, Miss S Sagendorf, A M Mann, large afghan.

Miss Maggie Reed, toilet cushion, mat, box, doll's things.

Miss Florence Jones, sofa cushion.

J H Hickok, books, &c., $60 04.

L. M. Arnold, old Dutch Bible.

No Name, bunch flowers, 6 scent bags, 7 mats, 3 tidies, 4 cushions, 6 book marks, 10 boot pin cushions, needle book, 3 parlor balls, slippers, 6 cigar holders.

Miss Van Rensselaer, cushion, 2 pairs infant's socks, 2 toilet sets.

Ralph Bailey, 150 spools of silk.

Miss H Lockwood, 3 pairs slippers.

Miss Shows, pair of gent's socks.

Mrs Robt N Palmer, child's sack, cus'n.

Miss Nettie Chamberlain, 6 yokes and sleeves.

Clara Buys, 2 bead collars.

Mrs T S Lloyd, coverlid.

Mrs Charles Underwood and Miss E Underwood, 2 pairs children's drawers, mat, book mark, cushion.

Miss Humphrey, mat, watch case, 3 pen wipers, 4 cushions.

Mrs A H Wright and family, crochet collar, pair socks, 2 holders, 6 pen wipers, 2 cus'ns, 2 Persian silk aprons, 4 tooth picks, napkin rings, 5 crosses and 5 silk winders made of the wood from John Bunyan's house.

Miss E Thomas' table, 2 cus'ns, 3 watch cases, toilet set, 2 hoods, rigolette, neck tie, 8 pocket pin cushions, inf's socks, 2 pen wipers.

No Name, sontag.

Miss E A Place, cuffs, collar, pin cush'n.

Miss A K Vail, 2 pairs drawers.

Miss Babcock, knitting apron, 2 watch cases, 4 pin cushions, neck bows, basket cushion, pair wristlets, 3 scent bags, spool bags.

Nettie Van Wyck, pin cus'n, perfumery bags, book mark, 6 cro ses.

Mrs Major Smith, chil l's sack, 2 child's aprons, sofa cushion.

Miss Libbie Smith, 2 knit shirts.

Maggie Smith, pair lines.

Miss Mary A Ferris, frame box, needle book, 2 pin cushions.

Miss Ellen Sterling, piano stool cover, handkerchief holder.

Mrs Wm C Sterling, 2 shirts, slippers, sack, needle book, 2 shirts, 2 doll's suits, 2 pin cushions, pen wipers.

Mr Simmons, slippers, mittens.
Mrs Milton Hare, Washington, 8 spectacle wipers.
Miss J A Smith, Washington, box wax flowers.
Miss H Smith, box wax flowers.
Mrs Lawrence, 2 tidies.
Miss Carrie Holman, Beekman, pin cushion, 2 watch cases.
Mrs Johnson, Red Hook, watch case.
Miss Eliza Johnson, tidy.
" Sarah Boyne, slippers.
Mr Vassar, 25 photographs.
Mrs Filkins, 2 chairs.
Miss Mary White, 2 work bags.
Mrs S ward, doll, doll's chemise.
" Spencer, bonnet.
Miss M Clapp, Pleasant Valley, tidy.
" Tobey, pair birds.
" Ward, net.
" Smith, net.
" DeGarmo, Hibernia, 2 mats.
" Townsend, cushion.
" Eliza Lawrence, mat.
" Anna Nelson, cushion.
" Ada Nelson, mat.
Mrs Dr Buel, 2 prs stockings, infant's shirts, 2 book marks.
Mrs G K Lyman, mat, needle book, scissor case, 3 cushions, work basket.
No Name, 2 pyramid pin cushions, 2 kitchen cushions, 4 doz'n pen wipers, mus-lin apron, smoking cap.
A Friend, 3 cards aut unn leaves.
Miss H M Coffin, worsted tidy.
" Mary A Cloy, collar and cuffs.
" Mary Coffin, 7 pocket cushions.
" Carrie Coffin, book mark, 6 pairs infant's socks.
Miss Gertrud Myers, Hackensack, yoke and sleeve.
Mrs E H Parker, breakfast shawl, 2 int's sacks, 2 dolls.
Lindley M Ferris & family, 7 cases; 84 photographs; 3 lamp shades; worsted slippers; 3 small dolls; 3 cross book marks; pocket pin cushion; 2 parlor balls; infant sack; 6 pen wipers; 2 needle books.
Mrs W W Cornell, 10 butterfly p wipers.
Miss Eliza Herriman, slippers.
George Peters, slippers.
Miss Fanny Clark, slippers.
" Helen Phillips, yoke and sleeves.
Mrs E M Owen, Pleasant Valley, 6 calico bibs; bouquet; moss pyramid; vest.
Miss Sarah Platt, head basket.
Mrs Thomas Lawrence, 10 pen wipers; 1 pin cushions; mat; 2 bead collars; basket; 4 shoe pin cushions.
Mrs Charles Lawrence, 2 mats; cushion.
Miss Irene Beach, infant sack; pr socks; 2 mats.
Miss Louisa Beach, slumber roll.
No Name, 2 pair gent's socks; 2 mats; bag.
Miss Emma Corlies, tidy; pin cushion; shoes; lines.
Miss Minnie Corlies, pair lines.

Mrs Jacob Corlies, 2 work baskets; 2 spool wagons; 2 holders; 3 inf't shirts; 2 tidies.
Mrs Geo Corlies, infant sack; 6 scarfs; breakfast shawl; slippers.
Mrs Samuel Mott, quilt.
" Tillotson, Cincinnati, 3 pocket hdkf holders.
Mrs Holmes, embroidered suspenders.
Miss Fannie Clark and Jennie Degroff, 6 doll's riding hoods; 1 dozen rabbits; 3 fancy collars; 2 card cases.
Miss Merritt, invalid's slippers, mittens, 2 b'k marks, 4 doll's cloaks, 2 tidies, watch case.
Mrs Wm A Davies, 3 hoods.
No Name, 4 pairs worsted wristlets.
Ladies of the Locust Glen Aid Society, 4 traveling boxes.
Miss Van Wyck, New Hamb'h, 3 ducks, 5 cards raisin turtles, 4 scent bags, slippers, 2 needle books, brioche, 2 sofa pillows.
Mrs Stockholm, 2 bunches feather flowers.
Miss Minnie and Katie Hopkins, 3 parlor balls.
East Fishkill, 3 yokes and sleeves, 2 night caps, pin cushion, pair mats, 10 pocket cushions, pair lines.
Miss Gertrude Matthews, 8 prs infant's socks, doll's socks, cloud.
Mrs John H Matthews, 5 breakfast caps, mice.
Miss Sarah P Adriance, ladies' friend, pin cushion, pen wiper, baby's scarf, pair bottles and mats.
Miss Anna V Adriance, cush'n, 2 dolls, pen wiper, doll's afghan.
Miss Kittie Kettell, breakfast shawl.
Mrs Geo Jones and family, 8 cushions, 30 pocket pin cushions, 12 shaving cases, 4 needle cases, 26 pen wipers, 3 pairs slippers, 2 work bags.
Rev Mrs Sleight, 5 cushions, 4 pocket cushions, purse, bib, tidy, 2 pairs gauntlets.
Mrs S Odell, 11 tomato cushions, mat, 2 pocket cushions.
Mrs Thomas Allen, $5 00.
" J H Odell, $9 00.
" Jos'h Bowers and family, 4 pounds white wool, 2 mats, spool holder, needle book, 2 pin cushions, 5 pocket cushions, 2 bows.
Miss M Kinney, sack, 3 needle cases, watch case, 2 cushions.
J G Wood & Co., articles, $70 20.
Miss Van Keuren, Pleasant Plains, what not.
" Kate M Losee, Washington, cus'n.
" Phebe T Losee, 1 set toilet mats.
Mrs James Winslow, a bride.
James Winslow, case birds valued $100, fancy jewelry, $200.
Miss Thompson, child's talma, 2 knitting bags, 4 pairs of slippers, pin cushion, pr mats, 3 cigar cases, 6 paper folders, 21 pocket cushions.

T Wright, 100 contrabands, 12 rustic frames, Jeff Davis' dream, small turtles.

Mrs Jones, basket of mottoes.

Miss Julia Jones, book-mark.

" Carrie Barlow, Washington, set of toilet mats.

Miss L B Coffin, pair watch cases, 2 needle books, mats.

Miss Lizzie Coffin, worsted tidy.

" Mary Coffin, 2 cushions, pair cotton stockings.

Miss Maggie Coffin, cushion.

Friend, bead collar, scarf, hanging cushion.

Soldiers' Friend, pair mats.

Mrs. Sutherland, worsted mat.

Mrs. Mosher, sewing apron.

Miss Mabbett, sewing apron.

" Frank Smith, 3 pictures in cone frames, anchors, crescent and cross in moss.

Mrs. James Clark, basket of pocket cushions.

Miss J. Clark, bachelor's pin cushion.

" Rebecca North, 2 pictures.

Mrs. Barker, 4 caps, 2 head dresses.

Miss Ellie Swift, crochet scarf, worsted mats.

Mrs Spencer, bonnet.

Miss Deborah Tobey, mat.

Mrs Stephen Bull, boquet of japonicas.

Miss Lucia L Booth, pin cushion.

" Mary Parmentier, 2 dolls, pen wipers.

Miss Lydia Parmentier, velvet cushion.

" Lucy Trivett, 3 worsted hoods.

" Nichols, 2 pairs woolen stockings.

Lottie Wood, 2 sets of lines.

Mrs. Robert Taylor, slippers, collar, 12 tomato cushions.

Mrs S B Wheeler, breast pin and ear rings.

Miss Carrie Frost, Pleasant Plains, shaving papers and dressing case.

Darrow & Son, 4 caps, lady's skating cap, set of children's furs.

Mrs Dr. C. N. Campbell, Standford, slippers.

Mrs Leonard Campbell, mam'th lemon.

Miss Maria Wood, mat.

" Sarah Sands, 2 Quaker pin cush'ns.

Mrs J W Holman, work basket, 3 mats, moss cord, 4 pen wipers.

Miss Hendrickson, cushion.

E C Winter, 3 pictures.

Mrs Brown, lace collar.

" Sage, neck yoke.

Lieut Palmer, foot-stool taken from Gen Mills' house in Virginia.

Mrs C S Van Wyck, sofa cushion.

" E A Hitchcock, shell basket and pen wiper.

Richard Southwick, 7 leather breastplates for the bachelors of 1864.

Levi Mahado, 2 baskets of wax fruit.

Miss Southard, moss pyramid.

Mrs D W Mulford, pair mats.

Miss Horton, East Fishkill, 2 sets toilet mats, 2 pen wipers, 4 tiny mats.

Miss Ruth Flagler, Lagrange, 2 bead mats.

Miss Kate Southwick, pin cushion, what not, book mark.

Mrs D W Mondell, tidy, child's chemise and flannel shirt.

Mrs Richard Adriance, child's chemise.

" Raub, cushion, pair mats.

From Young America Engine Co. No. 6, Union dress cap and scarf.

Jane Davis, Reynolds, cone basket, pair mats, 25 pocket cushions, toilet cushion, worsted ball.

Miss Tompkins, pin cushion.

Mrs Wm H Crosby and daughters, sofa cushion, 4 pin cushions, 2 fortune tellers, 3 bonbon boxes, 6 enigmatical dinner parties, small carved easel, 3 letter holders, 2 watch cases, 2 satchels, 2 knit hoods, 3 infant's sacks, 7 enigmatical dining tables.

Mrs James Roosevelt, 10 satchels.

Mrs J T Dubois, Hudson, 2 tidies, 2 dolls, bag, 2 sacks.

The Widow's Mite, 1 doll.

Miss Harloe, 2 tidies, 6 perfume bags, 4 mats.

Mary A Hicks, 3 pin cushions, needle book, 2 book marks, 2 pocket cus'ns.

Jennie Hasbrouck's club, 6 mats, 2 b'k marks, 10 pocket pin cushions.

Silberstien & Co., 4 pairs stockings.

Miss Maggie Hyde, chair tidy.

" S Hughson, 2 hoods.

" J Hughson, cushion, pair mats, 8 pocket cushions.

Miss Tompkins, and Miss Mary T Merritt, 2 cush'ns, 3 pairs socks, 2 needle books, hood, scarf from an old lady.

Miss Barrett, 3 spool holders, collar, 3 pairs sacks.

Miss Osborne, 2 mats, 3 nut bags.

Mrs O W Booth, pen and ink sketch, book mark.

Miss Mary Jane Bailey. 6 bead mats.

Mr. Cleveland, books.

Mrs Hulm, 1 pair suspenders.

Mrs B J Lossing, 1 sofa cushion.

Invalid Soldier, bead work.

Mrs. J H. Coggswell,

" G. T. Brown,

" James Reynolds,

" Degroff,

" W. S. Wright,

" J. F. Hull,

" R. James,

" Boardman.

Report of Refreshments

Received at the "SANITARY FAIR," with names of the Donors.

POUGHKEEPSIE—Mrs C Dubois, jar pickles, 5 dozen eggs, 4 quarts beans; Mrs C J Howell, jar pickles, 2 cans cherries, can peaches; Mrs DeGarmo, 200 pickles in vinegar; Mrs Mary Lacy, 5 pounds granulated sugar; 2 papers cocoa; Mrs N Seaman, 7 pounds crushed sugar; Miss E Monfort, cake; B H Hart, basket crullers; Mrs Reed, boiled Ham; Mrs Bedell, maple syrup; Mrs G C Burnap, box Havana and box Sicily oranges, 100 quarts milk; Miss L DeGarmo, lady apples; Mrs Dewitt Clinton Jones, beef a la mode, 2 forms jelly; J McLean, 2 hams worth $8.20; Mrs E R Pease, pound cake; L Carpenter & Sons, 10 pounds Osborn's coffee, can spiced salmon, 6 bottles horseradish, 6 cans tomatoes, 4 cans peaches, box oranges, bottle Worcestershire sauce, 2 bottles pickles, 2 bottles cherries, 2 bottles catsup, 2 pounds chocolate; Edward Haight, 5 pounds coffee, 2½ pounds black tea, ham; Miss Annie E Frost, 8 bottles catsup; Mrs Cartwright, 6 jars apple jelly; Mrs Orrin Williams, 4 tongues and cake; Mrs Booth, 2 jars pickles; Mrs Wm Frost, 2 ornamented cakes; Mrs B B Reynolds, cake; Mrs R Taylor, 4 jelly cakes; Mrs Clarkson Underhill, pot of butter, 50 eggs, 20 quarts milk; Mrs Horn, pot of pickles, cake; Mrs Parker, 3 jars pickles; Mrs Emott, 12 Charlotte russes; Mrs G W Vail, glass bowl, kisses and maccaroni; Mrs LeGrand Dodge, basket biscuit and cake; Mrs S K Darrow, jr., jelly cake, cup cake, raisin cake, and sandwiches; Miss Laura Coffin, fancy cake; Mrs St. John, loaf sugar; Mrs Bogardus, pot of pickles; E H Crosby, basket lettuce, milk and cream; Mr Costar, milk; Mrs Yelverton, 50 biscuits; Mrs Geo Hull, jelly cake and sandwiches; Mrs Robert B Monell, Hudson, Columbia County, very large plum cake elegantly decorated; Mrs O S Atkins, crullers and biscuit; Mrs Dolson, waffles; Mrs Deyo Smith, sugar and coffee; Mrs Currier, sponge and nut cake; Carpenter & Bro.'s, 10 pounds java coffee, 2 pounds black tea, 1 pound green tea; Mrs John Disbrow, fruit cake; Mrs Schram, dish of trifles and mountain cake; A Friend, large piece beef a la mode; Leonard Winslow, bag of lady apples; Mrs Chas White, 4 loaves bread; Mrs Wm M Hill, ornamented pound cake; A Lady, pound and mountain cake, 6 dozen eggs; Nathan Gifford, 9 bottles currant wine 12 years old; A Peverelly, fancy sugar pyramid; E G Hopkins, 72 pounds crackers, 5 loaves bread; Mrs Wickes, apples; Kuhn & Palmer, an ornamented ham weighing 28 pounds; Mrs Gilbert Wilkinson, Garden street, raisin cake and 31 small cakes; Mrs Bech, 5 pounds fancy cake, 2 ornamented cakes, boned turkey; Mrs John Thompson, 4 cocoanut pies, 2 Charlotte russes; Mrs M J Myers, 4 loaves bread, cake; Mrs E Kuhn, cake; Mrs John A Storm, Delmonico pudding; Mrs H W Shaw, an ornamented cake; Mrs Eldridge, 3 cocoanut cakes; Mrs Dr Harvey, 4 fancy jellies; Mrs D B Lent, 5 quarts milk; Mrs Dr Babcock, biscuit each day during the Fair; Mrs James Reynolds, frosted cake; Mrs Moseby, biscuit; Mrs Wm A Davies, 2 boned turkeys; Mr Bower, piece smoked beef; Mrs Geo Van Kleeck, Charlotte russe; Mrs Richard Greenalch, marble cake; Mrs J B Sherman, biscuits and ½ dozen cans peaches; J B Jewett, 500 oysters; Mrs R F Johnson, biscuit; R High, ornamented cake worth $15, ten of which he donated, the other five Mrs T L Davies paid; Mrs Sydney Fowler, tapioca pudding; Wm Frost & Son, 2 milk cans; Mrs Cornelius Pugsley, turkey; Mrs Dr Babcock, cream puffs; Mrs Abele, fancy cake, 2 loaves bread; Mrs T L Davies, 6 forms jelly, dish baked apples; Mrs Thos Wheeler, canned cherries, peaches, 2 bottles wine; Mrs Charles W Swift, 21 forms jelly; Mrs Albert, basket carnival cakes; Mrs Sarah Rowe, fancy pyramid; Mrs Weddle, chocolate cake; Mrs Dr Andrus, biscuit, ham, and plate of kisses; Mrs Samuel Mott, pail crullers; Mrs J W Collins, basket biscuit; Mrs Wm E Beardsley, corn bread; Mrs I Platt, 14 pounds coffee crushed sugar; Mrs F Phinney, 2 dishes syllabub; Mrs Newcomb, basket cake; Mrs R Southwick, nut cake; Mrs Lawrence, 4 quarts milk each day of the Fair; Mrs Robinson, 2 tongues, biscuit; Mrs Buckingham, gallon milk; Mrs G V Wilkinson, cocoanut and chocolate cake; Mrs Gale, 4 forms lemon jelly; Mrs S H Bogardus, 2 cakes; Mrs Abel, jelly cake; Miss M A Van Valkenburgh, jelly cake; Mrs Phillips, cake and biscuit; Mrs Marble, ham and tongues; Miss Harriet Van Kleeck, 2 moulds of jelly; Mrs Edward Beach, cocoanut cake, loaf bread; Mrs Wm White, biscuit; Mrs Shaw, loaf bread; Mrs Jacob Degroff, basket biscuit; Mrs Nathan Gifford, 2 moulds jelly, cake; Mrs Dr Varick, cake, dish jelly; Mrs Dow, biscuit and 2 cakes; Mrs Tooker, 3 pies; Mrs Collingwood, piece of beef; Mrs Dr Babcock, 6 marmalade pies, cream cakes and apple puffs; Mrs George Corlies, ham, 5 mince pies, sponge cake; Mrs John Ward, 4 jars currant jelly; Mrs Rosekrans, 6 pies, biscuit; Miss Germond, chicken salad; Mrs Daniels, 4 mince pies; Mrs J Thompson, 2 Charlotte russes; Mrs Aaron Frost, cake and biscuit; Mrs Wm Smith, 6 pies; Mrs L B Sackett, cake; Mrs T L Davies, ham; Miss Trowbridge, wine jelly; Miss T Gill, 40 quarts milk; Mrs Jacob Sleight, 2 cakes; Mrs J C Pudney, cake and sandwiches; Mr Rowland, ornamented pound cake with a ring in it, ring contributed by Wm S Morgan; Miss Pardy, rice pudding; Mrs Winans, biscuit; Mrs Merritt, sandwiches, lemon jelly cake and crullers; Miss Strong, cake; Mrs S B Johnson, 2 cakes; Mrs Farnum, sandwiches; Carpenter & Bro.'s, 35 pounds butter; Mrs W W Cornell, cornuco- pias; Mrs Caleb Bishop, cucumber pickles; Mrs Patton, 2 ornamented cakes; Mrs Booth, 4 chickens; Mrs Geo Cornwell, ham; Mrs Thomas Parish, 4 cakes; Mrs F W Van Wagner, cake and biscuit; A Friend, fruit cake; Mrs Bunting, pound cake; Mrs Geo Van Kleeck, sandwiches and cake; Mrs Parker, cake and pies, 2 chocolate cakes; Mrs E Wright, 3 cakes and biscuit; Geo Gifford, a nice cake; Mrs W Corlies, 2 loaves bread, cake; Mrs Jas Reynolds, 3 cocoanut pies, chocolate cake, 2 merangue pies; Mrs C Bowne, 12 Charlotte russes; Mrs W H Tallmadge, bread and rum jelly; Mrs Jno McLean, biscuit rusk; Mrs T S Wickes, bread and biscuit; Mrs Geo Perrin, 3 cakes; Mrs Charles Underwood, cake; Mrs Walters, popped corn; Miss Maggie Livingstone, fruit and plain cake; Mrs John- son, fancy cake; Mrs Sackett, ham; Eben Cary, roasting piece of beef; Daniel C Rowe, 10 dozen eggs, bag walnuts; Mrs Buckingham, citron, pound and sponge cake; Mrs Lockwood, pound cake; Mrs Henry Seaman, 2 custard pies; Mrs J D Wilbur, 2 cakes, popped corn; N Lamoree, biscuit and crullers; Mrs Dr Flagler, biscuit; Mrs Anna, jar peaches, ½ dozen eggs; Mrs Augustus Thompson, cake; Mrs Junius Sterling, lemon pie; Miss M R Merrit, lemon pie; J R Lent, pail of milk; Mrs Booraem, biscuit and cake; Mrs Jacob Storm, cake; Mrs Richard Pudney, biscuit; E G Hopkins, 5 loaves bread, loaf of brown; Mrs Storm, cake; Mrs Tooker, bread; Mrs M P Jewett, sponge and lady cake; Mrs Wm A Davies, turkey; Mrs Rob't Slee, pudding; Mrs Duncan, sandwiches; Mrs J Reynolds, cake, Mrs R Palmer, biscuit and cake; Mrs J Lawrence, 2 pounds sugar; Mrs Bucking- ham, citron cake, boiled ham, gallon milk; Mrs George Innis, basket apples; Mrs Hull, cake and biscuit; Mrs Hitchcock, cake and bread; Miss Mosher, cake; Mrs J F Hull, biscuit; Mrs Henry Varick, cake and jelly; Mrs T S Wickes, 5 pies; Mrs Robert Taylor, ham and tongue; Mrs N Hill, cake; Mrs Herrick, sugar; Mrs C J Howell, 10 dozen eggs; Mrs Costar, milk and bread; Mrs Casper D Smith, 6 pies; Miss Lydia Arnold, cake, 2 forms jelly; E G Hopkins, 5 loaves bread; Mrs Overton, biscuit; Mrs Lockwood, turkey, 6 forms jelly; Mrs Henry Carew, rice pudding; Mrs H G Eastman, 2 cakes and sandwiches; Mrs H W Shaw, 2 sponge cakes; Mrs Wm W Reynolds, 2 pies; Mrs Grant, cake and biscuit; Mrs Monfort, cake; Miss Barrett, biscuit and pumpkin pie; Miss Julia L Clark, cocoanut cake with ring in it, ring contributed by Wm H Van Keuren; Mrs T L Davies, 6 forms jelly; Mrs Wm H Tallmadge, loaf bread; 2 bottles tomatoes; Miss Anna Frost, 4 loaves bread; Mrs Bower, 7 pies, 6 dozen eggs; Mrs Dr Harvey, 3 forms of jelly; Mrs James Freer, 2 cakes; Mrs John P Adriance, dish of jelly; Mrs Dr Fowler, biscuit and cake; Mrs James Reynolds, 5 pies; Mrs H D Myers, cottage cheese; Mrs Thomas Lawrence, 3 loaves bread and biscuit; Mrs Caleb Morgan, cake; Mrs Edward Southwick, cake and biscuit; Mrs Longfield, biscuit; Mrs Anthes, cocoa- nut cake; Mrs Schuppan, 3 pies; Mrs R Haxby, tapioca pudding; Mrs N Chi- chester, cake; Mrs L M Vincent, bread and jelly; Miss Julia Hughson, Scotch cake; Mrs James Winslow, dish chicken salad; Mrs John A Bailey, cake, 3 jel- lies; Mrs E M Crosby, pail milk, pail cream; Mrs Wm Van Keuren, cake; Mrs Barnes, 3 cakes; Mrs Buckingham, 4 quarts milk; Misses Mary and Carrie Barnes, cakes; Mrs Wiley, pickles; Mrs Richard Pudney, doughnuts and biscuit; Mrs Abele, 2 loaves bread; Mrs E M Van Kleeck, turkey, biscuit; Mrs Lloyd, ice cream; Mrs Holmes, biscuit, 3 lemon pies; Mrs J F Hull, biscuit; Miss Martin, 1 forms jelly; Mrs Chatfield, biscuit; Mrs Wm Reynolds, ham; Mrs Nathan Gif- ford, 2 pies; A Friend, 200 pickled oysters; Mrs Longfield, 2 mince pies; Mrs Wm Smith, ½ dozen lemon pies; Mrs Chas Bowne, fancy ring cake, the ring, a handsome one, contributed by Mr Quintard; Mrs Wm H Tallmadge, 2 loaves of bread; Miss Harriet Frost, 3 moulds jelly; Mrs A M Farrell, crullers, blackberry and currant jelly; Mrs L L Hutchings, biscuit; Mrs Hull, small pound cakes; Mrs J aias Sterling, biscuit; Mrs Wm Cornwell, 2 raisin cakes, jumbles and 2 custard pies; Mrs Geo Van Kleeck, pail fancy cakes; Mrs Vermilye, biscuit; Mrs Costar, 4 quarts milk; Miss Mary Nelson, sandwiches, chocolate and jelly cake; Mrs Hull, pound cake; Mrs Chas Dubois, silver cake; Mrs Henry W Morris, 2 bask's cake; M S B ach, 118 quarts milk, 2 quarts cream; Mrs Buckingham, 4 quarts milk; Mrs Edward Crosby, 2 quarts cream, 7 quarts milk; Mrs Dr Hasbrouck, 3 moulds jelly; Mrs Babcock, cranberries; Mrs Joseph Wright, 4 mince pies; Mrs Wm Cornwell, sponge cake; Mrs H D Myers, 2 cans tomatoes; Mrs E Beach, loaf bread; Mrs Rutzer, 24 splendid Charlotte russes; Mrs Chas H Ruggles, 1 bushel oil cooks.

RHINEBECK—Pocahontas Engine Co, No. 2, 1 pounds tea, 10 pounds coffee, 10 pounds sugar, 6 pounds butter, 10 packages prepared rice, 5 packages chocolate, 1 piece flannel, lot stocking yarn, 1 dozen pairs cotton half hose, 1 dozen pairs woolen hose.

PLEASANT PLAINS—Mrs A Leroy, loaf cake, 6 lemon pies; Sarah M. Cooking ham, nut cake, apples; Catharine Traver, 12 pounds dried apples, jar pickles. Mrs D Merritt, 2 cans fruit; Mrs H Van Vliet, corned beef, stewed pears, apple sauce and crullers; Mrs M Harris, 5 pies; Mrs M Cookingham, 6 dozen eggs; Mrs S M Cookingham, 50 eggs, 2 quarts stewed cherries; Mrs S Hoyt, 8 dozen eggs, roasted chickens; Mrs E Sherriger, 4 chickens, box honey; Mrs S Hoyt, half barrel apples; Lewis Cox, bushel potatoes; Mrs P D Cookingham, barrel filled with apples, roasted chickens and biscuit, valued at $1 75.

STAATSBURG—Miss E W Mulford, sponge cake; Miss Mary Van Vliet, pickles, cake, apple sauce; Mrs David Mulford, piece larded beef.

BARRYTOWN—Mrs Bard, dozen roasted chickens, 1 cooked ham.

HUMUENIA—Mrs D S DeGarmo, pail pickles and jumbles.

NEW HACKENSACK—Mrs J Conover, 2 cakes, pair chickens, plate of tarts; Mrs Philip Vanderbilt, 4 dozen eggs, frosted cake; Mrs O W Angel, 5 dozen eggs; Miss M Jones, lady apples; J B Jones, ham; Mrs Rogers, cake, jar of pickle, bowl of jelly; Mrs Van Kleeck, 6 dozen eggs; Miss C Knapp, 2 delicate cakes, cocoanut cake, can of pickles; name not given, cake; Mrs Diddell, 8 quarts of cream, lemon jelly, wine jelly, lady cake, chocolate cake, chicken salad, eggs and butter; Mrs Knapp, turkey; Mrs Russell, 2 pies, currant cake, pound cake, waffles; Mrs H D Hoyt, mountain and nut cake, doughnuts; Mrs Milo Bird, sandwiches, lady cake and biscuit.

CLINTON—Mrs Wing, bottle cherries; Hiram Wallace, basket biscuit.

DOVER—Pan of baked pork and beans, large box of splendid canned fruit, butter.

MILAN—Miss C Best, cake, pair roasted chickens, 2½ dozen eggs; Mrs J S Ferris, pair roasted fowls; Mrs Henry Wilbur, 3 dozen biscuit, pair chickens, 2 dozen eggs; Mrs Story, 3 dozen eggs; Miss Ferris, 2 cakes, pair chickens, turkey, ham; Mrs H E Knickerbocker, 4 pounds butter.

PLEASANT VALLEY—Mrs Owen, jar pickles; Mrs John H Bates, 3 dozen eggs; Mrs George Bates, pail doughnuts; Miss Lottie Cash, biscuit; Miss Mary Allen, biscuit; Mrs Wile, cake.

PAWLING—Mrs Jonathan Akin, turkey, ham, jar pickles; Mrs Jane Kirby, cake, turkey; Mrs Geo H Taber, cake; Mrs Geo P Taber, 2 turkeys; O A Taber, hickory nuts; Mrs Alex Arnold, cake; Mrs B F Arnold, cake, 90 pounds cheese; Mrs Clarke Kirby, turkey; Mrs Walter Taber, 2 jars pickled peaches; Mrs Chas Wing, 2 bottles wine, 2 cans cherries; Mrs Edward Wanser, 2 turkeys.

STANFORD—Mrs Margaret Creed, box dried raspberries, can of currants; Mrs L Canfield, dried currants; Mrs Lewis Adsit, cake, tongue, 3½ dozen eggs; Mrs H Vail, boiled ham; Mrs Isaac G Sands, roasted turkey; Mrs Wm Smith, cake; Mrs Wm Bishop, 2 green currant pies.

UNION VALE—Mrs J H Collin, 2 chickens, jug cream; Mrs Z R Skidmore, turkey.

WASHINGTON—Height & Merritt, barrel beets, half bushel onions, 2 bushels Swedish turnips, form of apple jelly, jar sweet tomato pickles, half bushel of popped corn; half bushel of doughnuts; Mrs Milton, ham, lady apples, 2 cans of pickles; Silas Knapp, turkey, feather brushes; Mrs Simmons, 4 pies, 2 chickens; Mrs A H Collin, boiled ham; H R C, 1 turkey; Miss Lucy Collin, 13 dozen eggs; Mrs Sharpsteen, roasted turkey; Mrs Van Kleeck, cake.

EAST FISHKILL—Miss Bartow, loaf bread, pair roasted chickens; Miss Horton, large lot of cake, cracked walnuts and apples; Miss Brett, cake; Mrs Isaac Sherwood, ham; Mrs Dubois, turkey.

FISHKILL—5 mince pies, roasted turkey; Miss Caroline Van Wyck, 2 cans of brandy peaches.

FISHKILL LANDING—Hickory nuts.

LAGRANGE—Edward Flagler, 2 cakes, quantity of apples; Mrs R Veli, biscuit; Mrs John A Montfort, pound cake; Mrs C A Ward, fruit cake and eggs; Mrs J W Pettit, box of apples; Mrs E Pettit, butter, cake, 4 cans jelly; Mrs J. G. Pells, pickle, ham and cake; Miss Capp, basket cake; Mrs H B Hicks, 160 kisses, cake.

"The Receiving Committee" would explain the incompleteness of this "Report" by stating that our list was kept "under difficulties," truly confusion being not the least. If in some cases names and quantities be found incorrect we (for this reason) crave indulgence. A few articles only were apprized and numbered by the donors, compelling us to give of such a strictly correct account. It would afford us pleasure to be thus definite with the whole, but in the hurry and bustle of the time we found it utterly impossible either to count or affix prices.

Hoping these explanations will be quite satisfactory, this "Report" is respectfully offered.

S. WILKINSON,	E. N. MYERS,
E. PARISH,	M. VAN ANDEN,
S. H. SCHRAM,	S. SWIFT,

CONTRIBUTIONS FROM TOWN OF BEEKMAN FOR BEEKMAN TABLE.

Mrs Henry D Sterling, 6 moss baskets, 9 emerys, cake, 3 forms of jelly; Mrs Elmore Noxon, cake and jelly; Miss Mary W Noxon, cake and canned pears; Mrs Wm H Seaman, 7 pounds sugar; Mrs S V Rogers, 2 pairs socks; Mrs Thos Cypher, canned peaches; Mrs Emily Armstrong, 2 chickens; Mrs David Rector, butter and pickles; Mrs James N Asby, turkey; Richard Rodgers, chicken and apples; Mrs William Doughty, chickens; Mrs Susan F Knapp, table cloth; Mrs Wm W Haxton, cake and kisses; Mrs Benj Horton, jelly; Mrs Joseph Doughty, canned cherries; Mrs J H Cook, biscuit; Mrs Benj H Sisson, chickens. Mrs James C Sweet, biscuit and cake; Mrs Elnathan Miller, biscuit and cheese; Mrs Geo Flagler, ham; Mrs Elizabeth Noxon, chickens; Mrs Henry D Cypher, nuts; Mrs Alexander Baker, stockings; Mrs C Brill, tea and coffee; Mrs Geo Cornell, jar pickles; Mrs Egbert Rogers, jar pickles; Ryley C Corey, turkey; Elmore Noxon, ham; Miss Caroline E Holmes, pin cushion; Miss Julia Holmes, 2 watch cases; Mrs Jas G Holmes, 2 chickens. Mrs A M Hall, cocoanut cake.

LAGRANGE TABLE CONTRIBUTIONS.

Peter R Sleight, 2 barrels of apples, 2 turkeys, ham, quantity cake; Mrs J Abel, 20 quarts of milk, cake; Philip Flagler, 3½ pounds butter; C Barlow, 2 chickens, 4 pounds butter, 20 quarts milk, pickles; Annie Downing, cake; Mrs J A Monfort, cake; Mrs William Seaman, quantity cake; Mrs H Van Benschoten, 2 forms wine jelly, chicken salad, quantity cake; John P Kane, 3 dozen eggs; Dennis Crimmens, 6 dozen eggs, 4 gallons milk; Mrs H Pettit, biscuit, butter, cake, apples; Mrs John Brown, chicken, cheese; Miss E Brown, cake; Mrs John Cornell, quantity pickles, 2 pies, Mrs J Ward, quantity cake; Mrs R Velie, biscuit; Mrs David Ver Valin, 30 quarts milk, 3 fancy forms butter, 2 fruit cakes, ham, turkey, 6 pounds of butter, 7½ dozen eggs; J Shear, turkey; Mrs J W Storm, quantity cake; Mrs L D Todd, 6 dozen eggs; Mrs Peter Clapp, quantity cake, 3 lemon pies; a friend, 2 jars pickles, 6 pounds butter; John G Pells, ham, cake; Mrs Mary Hart, box lemons, quantity cake; Mrs G Sherman, cake, jar of pickles, floating island, flowers; Mrs David T Barnes, cake, pickles; Mrs Jonathan Flagler, biscuit, milk; Mrs Dolson, cake, Mrs Silas De Garmo, 12 quarts of cream, form farina, syllabub, cake; Mrs Geo Ayrault, turkey, 10 quarts of ice cream, cake, pies, bread; Gilbert Shepard, bushel walnuts, can milk; Mrs Philip Van Benschoten, cake; Miss Jane Van Benschoten, biscuit, cake, butter; Mrs Edward Flagler, cake and apples; Mrs William Sharpsteen, turkey; Mrs Grant, pie, quantity of kisses; Mrs Lewis Hutchins, quantity of biscuit; Mrs Lewis Hutchins, quantity of biscuit; Mrs John Thompson, form Charlotte Russe; Leonard Carpenter, 2 gallons cider; Mrs James Van Kleeck, 3 chickens, 3 pounds butter, 3 jars of pickled cabbage, 4 quarts dried fruit, 6 pies; Miss Nichols, quantity of cocoanut drops; Miss Edith Peckham, bouquet; Mrs Hiram Hitchcock, bouquet.

List of Articles

Donated to the SANITARY FAIR.

Poughkeepsie— G M Welker, 1 wood pipe; G M Welker, 1 china pipe and case; Mr Jonas, neck tie; G K Lawrence, black cassimere vest; W O Dryer, 2 coffee pots; Reidinger & Caire, 19 stone pots; Uhl & Husted, clothes wringer; R E Lansing, kitchen mop; Uhl & Husted, 4 nests spice boxes; Matthew Farrand, dozen small bird houses; Richard C Southwick, 4 roans and lining leather; M S Beach, 4 pictures; Robert High, stuffed cat skin; Maison & McGeorge, lot of groceries; Mrs Dewitt Clinton Jones, basket moss; Benson J Lossing, crayon sketch Van Kleeck House; W S Morgan, 4 tin coffee pots; tin boiler, 4 iron spoons; Mrs J D Robinson, flag of 1812; Mr Disbrow, 1 flag-staff; Joseph Bajer, 100 cigars; Jacob Degroff, a lot of soap; Wm E Beardsley, 4 hot bed boxes; J F Lansing, pair French kid slippers; Charles Franklin, amp'a; H B Seeley, 2 dozen carte de visite, 10 photographs; Philip Waiter, children's pocket books; Nicholas Waiter, box cigars; S B Reckard, pr ladies' gaiters; S H Maxon, box cigars; Wm Fanning, 3 dozen clothes lines, 24 dozen fish lines; Chas Crooke, 2 oil paintings; Mrs Geo B Lent, 2 autumn leaf pictures, 2 engravings; Fowler & Gillen, lot groceries; R Taylor, 3 dozen boxes magnetic ointment; Mr Wright, Hyde Park road, ble woolen rolls for kitchen; Haxby & Miller, marble lamb; Mrs James Winslow, basket flowers; D Scott & Co., box hard soap; H B Seeley, 11 photographs; Wm Van Anden, mowing machine; Jacob Degroff, box fancy soap; Storm & Wilkinson, case fancy pieces harness; Benj. H Hart, box moss; G B Gaylord, 2 boxes oranges; Stephen H Bogardus, invoice goods, trunks, &c.; Mrs Wm A Davies, 7 pots plants; Trowbridge & Co., 100 pounds ham; D S Mallory, small bureau; James Brothers, 2 clothes frames, horse rake; L M Arnold, Parrott gun shot; Misses Foster & Buck, saddle lamb; F Rondel, oil painting; The Author, 26 boot-jacks; Mrs R C Foster, 15 doz. lemon soda; Daniels & Briggs, 2 cullenders; J Bartlett & Sons, barrel crackers; J H Yelverton, straw cutter; Crosby & Tenney, spring overcoat; Edward Crosby, 25 pots plants; Thomas L Davies, deer's head and antlers; Van Valkenburgh & Brown, lot of soap, toilet articles, &c.; Isaac W White, Wood mowing machine; Payne & Fowler, case toilet articles; A Friend, barrel hickory nuts; S Armstrong, cider mill; C Underwood, barrel flour; L M Arnold, 2 bronzed watch cases; R C Andrus & Co., rocking chair; Commercial paint works, lot paint materials; Jas Winslow, jewelry, fancy articles, &c.; A Little Girl, Conn., newspaper of 1773, MSS. of 1790-1792; Ward & Carpenter, 5 pounds coffee; James O Washburn, 20 yokes; Mrs Charles Dubois, chinese kite; Arnold & Co., lot of chairs; A Friend, 3 bushels potatoes; Miss Carpenter, oil painting; Samuel Currie, 20 pots flowers; Mrs S F B Morse, lot flowers; Mr Bech, 16 pots flowers; Mr and Mrs Ewing, pilot boat; A Wilson, old inkstand; Mrs I M Toucey, oil painting; Mrs I M Toucey, Mr Bennet, plant; Mrs Jas Winslow, 3 pots flowers; Smith & Wickes, ½ barrel flour; Mrs Wm A Davies, lot cut flowers; Mrs Thomas L Davies, lot cut flowers; Hon James Emott, 7 steel engravings; Mrs Stuyvesant, 19 pots flowers, box cut flowers; Mrs T D Baxter, canary bird and cage; Mrs Blake, folding arm chair; Matthew Farrand, carnation plant; Miss North, picture; Vaughn & Burnham, ladies' spring cloak; Adriance, Platt & Co., Buckeye mowing machine; Employees of Adriance, Platt & Co., Buckeye mowing machine, extra; J E Allen, coffee pot, burnishing iron, &c.; Disbrow & Whipple, plough; E Cary, roasting piece beef; Charles Walters, coffee pot and tea pot; H Hofer, pastel painting; Mrs W H Merritt, 3 pairs deer's antlers, 4 maps Hud

-on River. American Tooth Co., 6 sets false teeth; Overbaugh & Co., doz.
plated forks; Miss Mary Brush, square gilt frame picture; Edward Merritt, 2 bushels potatoes; Coleman & Co., saw dust; R D Cornell, South
down sheep; Jacob Barth, 100 cigars; Mr Mc Kenny, patent rein holder
for wagons, with the right for Dutchess County to manufacture; Miss
Bella Smith, 3 dolls; John R Lent, "how are you, Bunker Hill?" Mr
Butler, Hyde Park road, 9 pots plants; John R Lent, order, ton plaster;
Mr Reynolds, order, 5 tons coal; Mrs Dr Beadle, floral cake; Manchester
Paper Mill, book paper; Booth Hose Co., peacock stuffed; Mr Biddle, 40
carte de visites; Mr Lessett, 3 English lop-eared rabbits; H A Reed, invoice books; S M Buckingham, by K Gardiner, gardener, boquet flowers;
Mrs T L Davies, pot flowers.
    RED HOOK —J Hendricks, 5 gross tobacco.
    FISHKILL Glenham Woolen Co., 63½ yards summer cloth; W A Van
Warenen, 3 boxes elderberry wine; Unknown, case crab apple cider, 1
dozen quarts; Unknown, 2 barrels apples; Miss Brinckerhoff, pattern of
fern leaves; Wm H Van Voorhees, barrel of apples; Mrs Wm Verplanck,
barrel of provisions; Charles Dubois, lot of nursery trees.
    WASHINGTON—James M Thorn, sett of wagon rims, 2 setts wagon
thills; Haight & Merritt, bag rutabagas, bag onions.
    UNION VALE William Coe, box honey; R L Coe, barrel of apples.
    AMENIA Miss Kate Powers, 2 pictures in oil.
    LAGRANGE—H E McCord, 4 dozen eggs; David Ver Valin, 2 bushels
potatoes; James F Sleight, barrel flour.
    CLINTON—Mrs P D Cookingham, barrel chickens, &c.; S Hoyt, half
barrel apples; A A Underhill, barrel apples.
    MILTON Isaac S Hallock, 4 dozen champagne cider.
    PAWLING Lois E Marsh, painting on glass.
    HYDE PARK —Jonas Briggs, 2 boxes maple syrup, box hickory nuts;
Morris Traver, flour and meal.
    STAATSBURGH Wm B Dinsmore, tin box flowers.
    BARRYTOWN Mrs Bard, 9 boquets flowers; Mrs Donaldson, 4 baskets
flowers to Mrs Ruggle.
    PLEASANT VALLEY George Vandewater, 3 bushels potatoes.
    AMENIAVILLE Mrs Jones, oil painting.
    RED HOOK John C Cruger, box flowers.
    PAWLING Mrs T C Campbell, corner bracket ; Miss Clows, oil painting.
                        CORNELIUS VAN WYCK,)
                        JOHN R. SLEIGHT,   } Rec. Com.
                        EDWARD BURGESS.   )

List of Articles

Loaned to the SANITARY FAIR.

POUGHKEEPSIE M Vassar & Co., large flag; R Slee, large flag; James
E Wood, large flag; J Tice, 2 heater stoves; Daniels & Briggs, cooking
stove, 12 pounds pipe, Littlefeld burner and pipe, No. 6 stove, 22 pounds
pipe, iron pot, tea kettle, cook stove, 78 pounds pipe; William Frost &
Son, heater stove, small coal stove, cook stove; J E Allen, stove; Thomas
Coffin, heater stove; Hervey W Morris, desk in the office, desk for use of
treasurer, 4 hammers; James Brothers, hammer; Cleveland & Reed, 5
pictures; Albert Van Kleeck, flag; D H Dougliss, 2348 pieces crockery;
Reidinger & Caire, 135 pieces stone ware, &c.; Mrs E Van Valkenburgh,

2 flags ; Mrs Elsworth, flag, sword used in the Revolution ; Joseph Myers, picture of battle of Trenton ; Solomon B Wheeler, 2 flags ; Mrs Degroff, flag ; James G Wood, flag ; Mrs Colby, 2 gilt eagles, stuffed bird ; M S Beach, fortune teller, skating pond and fixtures, signs for tables ; Mrs Slater, soap plant from Bermuda Islands ; T D Baxter, gas star ; E C Winter, picture of Vassar College ; Trowbridge & Co., flag ; Theodore Allen, flag ; David Crockett Co., 3 flags ; Mary Smart, 2 pictures ; Mrs Robinson, 2 mirrors ; Nelson & Post, 3 marble top centre tables ; J G P Holden, autographs of different persons ; John S Slator, rebel parole returned ; First Reformed Dutch Church, flag ; Presbyterian Church, flag ; Johnny Colby, small black dog skin stuffed ; Robert Taylor, 2 flags ; H W Morris, wardrobe ; Engine Co. No. 2, flag ; C B Warring, flag ; Joseph E Allen, flag ; James Post, flag ; Mrs Dr Ebstein 2 large china vases and flowers ; W S Wright, sword captured from a member of the celebrated black horse cavalry ; Wm A Fanning, 3 flags ; Joseph G Frost, flags ; Mrs James Winslow, sword ; Mrs John P Adriance, flag ; John H Matthews, flag ; George Hannah, flag ; Wm Stevens, 3 oil paintings, 2 lithographs, map of Dutchess county ; Mrs L Thurber, punch bowl 150 years old ; J H Mathews, 3 sheets ; Matthew Farrand, oval case of curiosities ; Reynolds & Co., 7 flags ; R G Frost, picture ; Wm H Talmadge, picture ; Henry Frost, camp stool ; Mrs Wing, 2 camp stands ; Mrs Dobbs, picture of Washington and his generals ; R G Frost, 2 pictures ; Poughkeepsie ferry boat, 3 flags ; Nelson & Post, 57 camp stools ; S Gould, 6 pieces continental money ; Mrs Dr Beadle, large gilt looking glass ; Capt F J Miller, flag ; Smith & Sons, 6 marble top tables ; Thomas Clegg, 2 flags ; Foster & Gellen, flag ; George Wilkinson, 7 pictures and 1 oil painting ; Mrs Sterling, picture ; Mrs T L Davies, iron plate stand ; Mrs Sanford, 3 pictures ; City Hall, 4 chairs, 5 benches ; Edward Beech, 1 dozen pails ; J C Babcock, flag ; Mrs G Bailey, commission of Mr Bailey, confederate $100 bill, 2 trophies of the war, 1862, piece flag staff Marshall house ; Miss M Beardsley, 3 pictures ; R G Frost, 2 oil paintings ; Nathaniel Palmer, battle flag of the 130th Regiment ; Mrs Ward, looking-glass ; Resher & Co., flag ; Robert W Frost, 2 damask curtains ; Miss Blanchard, pastel drawing ; John Davies, flag ; Wm H Tallmadge, flag and lamp ; John McLean, flag ; F Rondel, 2 oil paintings ; Louis Rondel, oil painting ; Joseph Flagler, stand 100 years old ; Mrs John McLean, teapot 160 years old ; Mrs Chandler, steel engraving ; Mrs Lamott, old-fashioned lamps and looking-glass ; B J Lossing, steel engraving ; Miss Beardsley, 2 oil paintings ; Mrs Eastman, 4 oil paintings ; Robert Sanford, 4 oil paintings ; Arnold & Co., 2 dozen chairs ; R C Andrus, 36 camp stools ; Noel H Congdon, large picture ; Mrs Charles Dubois, Chinese hut ; Chas Eastmead, case shoes ; Miss M Beardsley, picture fruit piece ; Mrs Parker, refrigerator ; Mrs Wilson, slave lash, rebel newspaper ; John P Adriance, model mowing machine ; Mrs Dr Andrus, slave whip from New Orleans ; Mrs O Booth, arched plant with gold fish ; R Frost, 2 canary birds ; Mrs Hager, 2 pictures, 2 looking-glasses ; Mrs Buckingham, camp kettle, 100 years old ; Mr Thompson, case likenesses ; Mrs Dr C H Andrus, alligator skin and a likeness of the rebel General Ashby ; Trowbridge & Co., 24 pails ; F W Davis, photograph of Rear Admiral Farragut ; George Clapp, flag ; E P Bogardus, case fancy articles, piece of rebel cloth ; H G Eastman, 3 tables ; G Gaylord, flag ; H Hofer, 2 pictures ; Mrs Dr Hasbrouck, picture of dog's head ; Mr Scarborough, 25 camp stools ; J Blanchard, pair platform scales ; J H Hickok, 2 square pictures ; Engine Co. No. 4, flag ; Ed Bartlett, rebel banner, rebel musket ; Mrs Col Patten, lot of Indian relics and curiosities ; T F Clearwater, penmanship picture of Lord's prayer ; Heath & Cramer, use of gas fixtures.

Hudson—Mrs Clark, 2 flags.
Fishkill—Mrs C Knapp, pewter platter for Dutch kitchen.
Hyde Park—Mis Wright, deer's head and antlers.
Beekman—Large Flag.

CORNELIUS VAN WYCK, ⎫
JOHN R. SLEIGHT, ⎬ Rec. Com.
EDWARD BURGESS, ⎭

The following correspondence explains itself:

RHINEBECK, March 15, 1864.

Mrs. JAMES WINSLOW—Dear Madam : Since April, 1861, the commencement of the present struggle, Pocahontas Engine Co. 2, of Rhineck, have sent from their company twenty-three of its members, and for their sustenance and benefit the company would ask you to please accept of the accompanying box of articles in their name, with the very best wishes for the success of the Fair, and more particularly for the success of our army and navy, now and forever.

We remain yours, truly,

GEORGE A. CRAMER, Chairman of Committee.

SANITARY HALL, POUGHKEEPSIE, March 17, 1864.

Mr. GEORGE A. CRAMER, Chairman, &c.—Sir: The ladies of the Sanitary Fair have received your note accompanying the generous present from Pocahontas Engine Co., of articles for the Fair, valued at $50; and we have read with admiration your brief record of the patriotic devotion to, and personal sacrifices for, our common country which that company has exhibited. We accept your gift with gratitude, and as almoners of your bounty for the suffering soldiers we cordially thank you and your associates.

MRS. CHARLES H. RUGGLES, Secretary.

——o——

MOWING MACHINE PRESENTATION.

POUGHKEEPSIE, March 15, 1864.

To the Managers of the Poughkeepsie and Dutchess County Sanitary Fair:

The undersigned, in behalf of the employees of Adriance, Platt & Co., beg leave to present to the Fair the accompanying Machine - Buckeye Mower No. 2 as an evidence of their good will and sympathy for those brave defenders of our country for whose benefit the Fair is held.

THOMAS S. BROWN, ⎫
JONAS W. SERVY, ⎬ Committee.
G. W. BAXTER, ⎭

POUGHKEEPSIE, March 16, 1864.

To Messrs. Brown, Servy and Baxter, Committee:

The ladies of the Dutchess County and Poughkeepsie Sanitary Fair accept with gratitude your very generous donation of a Buckeye Mower, and in the name of the suffering soldiers for whose benefit they are now laboring they cordially thank you for this testimony of your own benevolence and patriotism, and your appreciation of their services in the cause of our common country.

MRS. CHAS. H. RUGGLES, Secretary.

Remarks, &c.

The thanks of the ladies are due the Advisory Committee for appointing the committees of gentlemen, all of whom faithfully performed the various duties assigned them; also, for assistance from the time of their appointment until the close of the Fair. The report of the Committee to Mrs Winslow, President, contains a minute and satisfactory account of the measures taken by them to aid the ladies in their preparations for the Fair, and of donations and loans made to the Fair through them.

It is regretted that it has been necessary to limit the size of the catalogue (to prevent additional expense) and that the greater portion of the report as well as other interesting documents have been omitted.

The following extracts from the report show the prompt and business like manner in which the committee performed their duties:

"On the day after receiving notice of their appointment, the members of the Advisory Committee met and at once proceeded to nominate the committees of gentlemen to coöperate with, and aid, the managers in carrying out their plans." The names of these committees have already been given.

"DONATIONS, &c.—A Friend, 2½ tons coal; Dr. Deyo, white lead; Gillen's Express, 8 cartages; No Name, 3 cartages; Messrs. McKibben, Fitchett, Hill and Lewis gave use of two horse teams, each to draw evergreens.

Dudley & Thompson, Wm. C. Arnold, Collingwood & Son, D. C. Foster, loaned lumber for Sanitary Hall.

Prof. Eastman loaned 170 chairs and 11 large tables. Mr. Siever, table.

Mrs. Jones, of Clinton Point, gave two loads of evergreens delivered at Sanitary Hall.

Mr. Wm. H. Morris loaned 1 mahogany sofa, 1 glass book case, table, desk, &c."

Other articles are mentioned as loans or donations, but have been included in reports of receiving committees.

"In conclusion, the Advisory Committee beg leave to congratulate the ladies of the Dutchess County and Poughkeepsie Sanitary Fair Association on the auspicious opening and the highly satisfactory closing of the Fair without serious accident of any kind, and with a full treasury; and they would only add that, if, in the exercise of their discretionary powers, they have in any way trenched on the prerogatives of any of the committees of ladies, it has been done through ignorance and not from design."

WILLIAM THOMPSON,
T. B. COSTER,
C. J. BUCKINGHAM,
WALTER VAN KLEECK.
} Committee.

When any great cause has been before the public, and a whole community have exerted themselves for its advancement as was the case from the opening to the close of the Sanitary Fair, it is very difficult to particularize individual favors. Every assistance has been most gratefully received, and if public notice of any name is omitted, it is to be hoped that none will feel intentionally slighted. It is hoped that donations of every kind have been recorded, but there may have been instances in which articles were taken directly to the tables without having been presented to a Receiving Committee, and it was not possible for them to have been credited upon any list. We make a few

SPECIAL NOTICES

of favors and donations not included in the report of any committee:

The Poughkeepsie Gas Company donated 10,000 feet of gas for the use of Sanitary Hall.

Mr. E. B. Killey printed some notices of the Fair and some bills for use of restaurant without charge.

The Poughkeepsie and New Paltz Ferry Company ran their boat at a later hour than usual, and at reduced price, to accommodate visitors to the Fair.

Plants and cut flowers were received from Messrs. Bard, Dinsmore, Kelly, Boorman, Wheeler, Miller, Stuyvesant, Crosby, Buckingham, W. A. Davies, T. L. Davies, Curry, Hagerty, Newbold, Emott, Dow, Winslow, Donaldson, Beeb, Kent, Brinckerhoff, Vassar and Beadle.

The following gentlemen were of great assistance to the Decorating Committee at Sanitary Hall: John W. Davies, Chester Freer, Henry S. Frost, L. F. McDonald, F. Foster, Mr. Sterling, Mr. Luddington.

Mrs. Jones, of Clinton Point, and Mrs. Colonel Livingston, of Poughkeepsie, furnished the greens for decorating the Hall.

The different Receiving Committees merit particular notice for the faithful manner in which they discharged their arduous duties.

All who attended the Fair will remember the Floor Committee with grateful pleasure. Better selections could not have been made. Energetic in the performance of their innumerable duties, kind and polite to all, they devoted their whole time till the close of the Fair in rendering valuable aid where most needed, and ever acquitted themselves with honor.

(From the Daily Eagle, April 20th, 1864.)

The ladies wish to express their thanks to Mr. Johnston, Provost Marshal, for aid rendered them during the Fair, in procuring for them about 50,000 oysters of the best quality, at first cost prices, free of the charge for freight, &c. Also, for furnishing a cook for the same at his own expense.

By order of the President,

Mrs. JAMES WINSLOW.

CHAS. EASTMEAD'S

FAMILY SHOE STORE,

254 Main Street,

FIRST DOOR EAST OF THE CITY BANK, POUGHKEEPSIE,

MANUFACTURER AND DEALER IN

FIRST CLASS WORK OF EVERY DESCRIPTION,
SECOND TO NONE IN STYLE, QUALITY,
AND WORKMANSHIP.

Believing that our assortment cannot be approached elsewhere, either for variety, beauty of design, or exquisiteness of Workmanship: the four great features of our establishment being

Variety, Quality, Style and Economy,

OUR MOTTO BEING, NONE

CHEAPER, UNLESS INFERIOR.

LADIES AND GENTLEMEN HAVING TENDER FEET.

We beg leave to call the attention of such to our method of measuring by which we guarantee a fit, unprecedented for comfort, yet combined with the most Fashionable shape. Those on whom shoemakers have practiced unsuccessfully, are particularly solicited to give us a call.

C. EASTMEAD.

F. VAIL will be happy to see his friends and the public at this establishment.

S. V. FROST & SON,
INSURANCE AGENTS,
No. 10 Garden-st., Po'keepsie.

AGENTS FOR THE FOLLOWING COMPANIES: ·

Howard Insurance Company, New York.

| Capital and Assets, 1864, | $411,770 84. |
| HENRY A. OAKLEY, Sec'y. | SAMUEL T. SKIDMORE, Prest. |

Home Insurance Company, New York.

| Capital and Assets, 1864, | $3,000,000 00. |
| JOHN McGEE, Sec'y. | CHAS. J. MARTIN, Prest. |

Hartford Fire Insurance Company, Hartford, Ct.

| Capital and Assets, 1864, | $1,500,000 00. |
| T. C. ALLYN, Sec'y. | H. HUNTINGTON, Prest. |

Springfield Fire and Marine Insurance Co., Springfield, Mass.

| Capital and Assets, 1864, | $557,863 47. |
| WM. CONNER, Jr., Sec'y. | EDMUND FREEMAN, Prest. |

Atlantic Fire Insurance Company, Brooklyn, N. Y.

| Capital and Assets, 1864, | $394,948 71. |
| HORATIO DORR, Sec'y. | JOHN D. COCKS, Prest. |

Niagara Fire Insurance Company, New York.

| Capital and Assets, 1864, | $592,046 00. |
| T. NOTMAN, Sec'y. | JONATHAN D. STEELE, Prest. |

Arctic Fire Insurance Company, New York.

| Capital and Assets, 1864, | $605,504 07. |
| V. TILYOU, Sec'y. | J. WILSON SMITH, Prest. |

Security Fire Insurance Company, New York.

| Capital and Assets, 1864, | $1,400,000 00. |
| E. L. HAYDOCK, Sec'y. | JOSEPH WALKER, Prest. |

This Company allows its Customers to participate in the profits.
Scrip Dividend 1863—55 per cent. ·

Commerce Insurance Company, Albany.

| Capital and Assets, 1864, | $250,000 00 |
| G. A. VAN ALLEN, Sec'y. | A. VAN ALLEN, Prest. |

Manhattan Life Insurance Company, New York.

| Capital and Assets, over | $500,000 00 |

The above companies insure Stores, Dwellings, Manufacturing Establishments, Farm property, Mills, Merchandize, Furniture, and all other Insurable Property against Loss and damage by Fire, on the most favorable terms. Losses equitably adjusted and promptly paid.

HENRY S. FROST.   SOLOMON V. FROST, Agents.

DARROW & SON,
DEALERS IN
Hats, Caps, Straw Goods,
FURS, ROBES, &c.
No. 264 Main-St., Poughkeepsie.

DARROW & SON.
264 Main Street.
POUGHKEEPSIE. N. Y.

Have constantly on hand, and will sell as low as the market rates permit, a full assortment of

SILK HATS,	CLOTH CAPS,
SOFT HATS,	PLUSH CAPS,
CLOTH HATS,	GLAZED CAPS,
WOOL HATS,	FUR CAPS,

STRAW HATS and CAPS, for Men, Boys and Infants, of every style in vogue. Also LADIES FURS in their season, consisting of

CAPES,
    HALF CAPES,
        VICTORINES,
            EUGENIES,
                COLLARS,
                    MUFFS and CUFFS,

Of Mink, Sable, Siberian Squirrel, Marten and all other kinds that are worn.

CHILDREN'S FURS IN GREAT VARIETY.

They also keep a large stock of Gentlemen's Fur Gloves, Mittens and Mufflers. Buffalo, Wolf, Fox, Coon and other Fancy Robes. Buckskin Gloves and Mittens.

Dogskin Gloves for driving—lined and unlined.

Umbrellas of all grades.

Ladies Skating Caps and Mittens.

And every other article in their line that can be found in a first class establishment.

DARROW & SON desire to inform their patrons and others that it is not expected to sell to every one that looks at their goods ; but the goods will be freely shown ; and they flatter themselves that not only the articles but the prices will commend themselves to purchasers.

264 MAIN STREET.

N. B. The highest prices paid for Raw Furs

OVERBAUGH & DEDERICK,

DEALERS IN

GENERAL HARDWARE,

BUILDERS MATERIALS,

AGRICULTURAL IMPLEMENTS, &C.

ALSO MANUFACTURERS AND DEALERS IN

Guns,

Rifles,

Pistols,

Cutlery,

FISHING TACKLE,

AND

SPORTING IMPLEMENTS.

Repairing of Guns and Locks, fitting Keys, Bell hanging and all other work in our line promptly attended to.

CHAS E. OVERBAUGH. WM. H. DEDERICK.

WILLIAM B. WEST may be found at the old stand with Overbaugh & Dederick.

ALL PATTERNS OF FRUIT JARS

JOHN W. BARRATT, IMPORTER & DEALER IN CHINA, GLASS, EARTHEN WARE &c. 347 MAIN ST. POUGHKEEPSIE N.Y.

JOHN W. BARRATT, IMPORTER & DEALER IN CHINA, GLASS, EARTHEN WARE &c. 347 MAIN ST. POUGHKEEPSIE N.Y.

NOTICE.

One thing is sure, viz: The place to buy the handsomest and latest patterns of

Stone China
Tea,
Dinner,
and Toilet Sets

ever seen in this city is at

JOHN W. BARRATT & CO.'S,

(IN THE NEW BLOCK.)

A GREAT VARIETY OF COAL OIL LAMPS.

JOHN W. BARRATT, IMPORTER & DEALER IN CHINA, GLASS, EARTHEN WARE &c. 347 MAIN ST. POUGHKEEPSIE N.Y.

JOHN W. BARRATT, IMPORTER & DEALER IN CHINA, GLASS, EARTHEN WARE &c. 347 MAIN ST. POUGHKEEPSIE N.Y.

WILLIAM FROST & SON.

DEALERS IN

STOVES,

RANGES AND HEATERS.

TIN, COPPER, BRASS,

Sheet - Iron, and Brittannia Ware.

Japanned and Housekeeping Articles,

PUMPS OF ALL KINDS.

LEAD PIPE AND SHEET LEAD.

All orders for TIN ROOFS, GUTTERS, LEADERS, etc., executed in the best manner and with despatch.

AGENTS FOR

LILLIE'S BURGLAR AND FIRE PROOF SAFES.

291 Main Street,

Poughkeepsie, N. Y.

CORNER OF GARDEN.

WILLIAM FROST.   *R. W. FROST.*